United States Department of Agriculture

I0467336

Economic Research Service

www.ers.usda.gov

Access this report online:

www.ers.usda.gov/publications/err-economic-research-report/err17x

Download the charts contained in this report:

- Go to the report's index page www.ers.usda.gov/publications/
  err-economic-research-report/err172
- Click on the bulleted item "Download err172.zip"
- Open the chart you want, then save it to your computer

Recommended citation format for this publication:

Hertz, Tom, Lorin Kusmin, Alex Marré, and Tim Parker. *Rural Employment Trends in Recession and Recovery*, ERR-172, U.S. Department of Agriculture, Economic Research Service, August 2014.

Cover image: Shutterstock.

Use of commercial and trade names does not imply approval or constitute endorsement by USDA.

United States Department of Agriculture

Economic
Research
Service

Economic
Research
Report
Number 172

August 2014

Rural Employment Trends in Recession and Recovery

Tom Hertz, Lorin Kusmin, Alex Marré, and Tim Parker

Abstract

This report examines the effects of the recent major recession and gradual recovery on county employment and unemployment rates, with an emphasis on rural America. The recession was marked by a 6-percent contraction in nonfarm employment and a doubling of the national unemployment rate between 2007 and 2009. Geographic variation in both the employment effects of the recession and the pace of job growth during the recovery has been striking, with large differences between regions, between metro and nonmetro counties, and between more and less rural nonmetro counties. We document these geographic differences and analyze their causes, demonstrating the relative importance of factors such as the county's industrial composition, the age structure of the county's population, and the educational status of its workforce.

Keywords: Rural recession and recovery, local labor market outcomes, metro and nonmetro counties, population density, economic growth, unemployment, industrial composition.

Acknowledgments

The authors wish to acknowledge extensive and helpful comments on this work received from Mary Bohman, Robert Gibbs, David McGranahan, and Marca Weinberg of USDA, Economic Research Service (ERS); and three anonymous referees. We also thank ERS editor Dale Simms and ERS designer Cynthia A. Ray.

Contents

USDA United States Department of Agriculture

A report summary from the Economic Research Service

August 2014

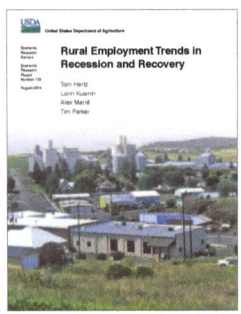

Find the full report
at *www.ers.usda.
gov/publications/err-
economic-research-
report/err172*

Rural Employment Trends in Recession and Recovery

Tom Hertz, Lorin Kusmin, Alex Marré, and Tim Parker

What Is the Issue?

In December 2007, 6 years of economic growth ended as the U.S. economy entered the most severe recession since the Great Depression. Eighty-two percent of U.S. counties experienced job losses as a result of the recession, but some places were hit much harder than others, and some have recovered more rapidly. This report describes the nature and causes of this geographic variation, which include differences in the mix of industries that support the local economy, in population growth trends, and in the demographics of the local workforce. How did these factors lead to differences in employment outcomes between urban (metropolitan) and rural (nonmetropolitan) areas and among nonmetro counties? What explains geographic differences in the severity of unemployment during the recession and the pace of job growth since the end of the recession?

What Did the Study Find?

National nonfarm employment fell by 6.3 percent from its peak in January 2008 to its nadir in February 2010. In May 2014, fully 5 years after the official end of the recession, the number of nonfarm jobs has finally reached its pre-recessionary peak level. Yet, given slow but steady population growth over the intervening years, the share of the adult population that was employed in May 2014 remains 4 percentage points below its pre-recessionary level and 9.8 million people (or 6.3 percent of the U.S. workforce) remain unemployed, 3.4 million of whom having been out of work for more than 6 months.

Regional differences in the effects of the recession are striking, with the column of States running from North Dakota to Texas faring much better in terms of employment and unemployment rates than most other regions. The Great Plains States in particular experienced smaller spikes in unemployment largely because their initial industrial composition was skewed toward relatively stable economic sectors (in particular, agriculture) and away from some of the hardest hit sectors (e.g., manufacturing).

Employment losses from their peak values were slightly larger in nonmetro than metro counties and began a year earlier, in 2007. Employment recovered over the course of 2010, growing at a comparable pace in metro and nonmetro counties. But nonmetro employment growth slowed in 2011 and fell to zero or slightly below thereafter. Our statistical analysis suggests that about half of this employment growth deficit is due to nonmetro counties having slower population growth. In addition, fewer jobs are being created in areas that have older and less well-educated workforces. Together, these effects outweighed the benefits of nonmetro counties' more favorable mix of industries, in particular their higher employment shares in agriculture and the robust extractive industries (mining, oil, and gas).

ERS is a primary source of economic research and analysis from the U.S. Department of Agriculture, providing timely information on economic and policy issues related to agriculture, food, the environment,and rural America.

The most rural nonmetro counties were less affected by employment losses and unemployment increases during the recession. Counties in the lowest population-density category saw average employment levels fall by just 1.3 percent during the recession, versus 5 to 6 percent for medium- and high-density nonmetro counties. Again, these differences were driven in part by differences in the local mix of industries. At the start of the recession, the more rural counties had much lower shares of employment in manufacturing, an industry that suffered some of the most rapid job losses during the recession. More rural counties also had higher shares of farm employment and Federal employment, sectors that, in general, did not shed jobs during the recession.

The employment effects of the recession were more pronounced in nonmetro counties with large African-American populations. These areas saw employment fall by 7.9 percent, compared to 4.1 percent for counties with no large minority populations. This pattern could not readily be explained by the types of industries found in counties with large African-American populations, by the educational status of their workforces, or by differences in age structure or prior population and employment growth trends. Instead, the most important explanatory factor appears to be that these counties were located in Southeastern States that lost employment across the board, in counties with both high and low African-American population shares. Still, when we include a county-level variable that measures the share of the population that is African-American, this variable is statistically associated with an average 1.3 percentage points of the excess job losses experienced by these counties. The causal mechanism behind this result is not clear. In particular, these results are not direct evidence of racial discrimination in the labor market, which cannot be assessed using county-level analysis such as this. Instead, race may be serving as a proxy for other measures of socioeconomic and labor market disadvantage that led to below-average outcomes during the recession. Regardless, these results provide evidence of a disparate impact of the recession on areas with large African-American populations, holding a number of other important factors equal.

Nonmetro counties with large Hispanic populations actually managed to *add* jobs during the recession (employment increased by 0.2 percent), and employment has grown by 4.6 percent during the 4 years of economic recovery, compared to 1.8 percent for nonmetro counties without large minority populations. Here, industrial composition proves most important; Hispanic counties had much lower shares of employment in manufacturing than did counties without large minority populations (5 percent versus 13 percent), which insulated them from the steep manufacturing employment decline. Although counties with large Hispanic populations continue to grow faster than average during the recovery, below average levels of educational attainment—as in counties with large African-American populations—have slowed employment growth during the 4-year recovery period.

How Was the Study Conducted?

The primary sources of data for this analysis were the Census Bureau's Current Population Survey and American Community Survey and the Bureau of Labor Statistics' Local Area Unemployment Statistics and Quarterly Census of Employment and Wages datasets. These were used for descriptive and multivariate regression analysis. Secondary sources were used in discussing macroeconomic trends, household debt burden, the causes and consequences of long-term unemployment, and other factors.

In interpreting this report's findings, two caveats need to be recognized. First, the report focuses exclusively on employment outcomes and ignores many other factors that influence economic well-being, such as wage levels, income, poverty, and other factors affecting living standards. A second important caveat concerns the multivariate regression analyses used in this study, the findings of which depend on the accuracy and specificity of the underlying data on county characteristics, and on the choice of regression specification, both of which have limitations. In particular, data on industry shares are available for all counties at only a fairly high level of aggregation, limiting their explanatory power. The regression specifications are chosen to work with the available data in order to shed light on some of the broad factors that may have contributed to geographic variation in employment outcomes. As always with regression analysis, their precision should not be overstated, and the possibility of biased estimation results cannot be dismissed.

Rural Employment Trends in Recession and Recovery

Introduction

In December 2007, 6 years of economic growth ended as the U.S. economy entered what would prove to be the most severe recession since the Great Depression. National nonfarm employment fell by 6.3 percent from its peak in January 2008 to its nadir in February 2010. In May 2014, 5 years after the official end of the recession, the number of nonfarm jobs finally reached its pre-recessionary peak. Yet, given slow but steady population growth over the intervening years, the share of the adult population that was employed in May 2014 remains 4 percentage points below its pre-recessionary level, with 9.8 million people (or 6.3 percent of the U.S. workforce) remaining unemployed, 3.4 million of whom having been out of work for more than 6 months.

Eighty-two percent of U.S. counties experienced employment losses between the fourth quarters of 2007 and 2009. This report documents the patterns of geographic variation in employment and unemployment trends during the recession and subsequent recovery, with a focus on rural America.[1] Nonmetro counties as a whole experienced earlier and slightly larger percentage declines in employment than did metro areas during the recession, and nonmetro employment growth has lagged metro growth during the recovery. However, among nonmetro counties, the most rural areas were less affected by recessionary employment losses and experienced smaller changes in the unemployment rate.

We document and analyze factors associated with counties' employment and unemployment changes, examining the recession and recovery separately, and framing our analysis around four main questions:

1. What explains why unemployment rates rose by much smaller amounts during the recession in counties located in the Plains States than elsewhere?

2. What explains the slow pace of employment growth in rural counties since the end of the recession?

3. Why did the least densely populated nonmetro counties, and those that were not adjacent to metro areas, generally experience smaller job losses during the recession?

4. What explains the differing employment outcomes observed during the recession and the recovery for counties with large African-American population shares and large Hispanic population shares?

---

[1]Many different definitions are used to capture urban/rural differences. See http://www.ers.usda.gov/briefing/rurality/whatisrural/. We use the June 2013 Office of Management and Budget classification of metropolitan (or metro) versus nonmetropolitan (nonmetro) counties, and will use "nonmetro" and "rural" interchangeably in this report when the meaning is clear.

Causes and Consequences of the 2007-09 Recession: A National Overview

The most immediate cause of the 2007-09 recession was the collapse of a debt-financed speculative bubble in real estate. The years leading up to the recession saw the longest sustained increase in housing prices since at least 1970. Between 1999 and 2006, the national average price of a single-family home doubled, and prices nearly tripled in some metro areas on the east and west coasts.[2] This appreciation was facilitated by, and in turn contributed to, the most rapid increase in household debt in postwar U.S. history. Between 2001 and 2008, the ratio of household debt to disposable income increased by about 5 percentage points per year, rising from 97 percent to 133 percent; by contrast, the average rate of increase over the previous 40 years was just 1 percentage point per year. This borrowing drove the ratio of annual savings to disposable income down to 2.2 percent during 2005-07, compared to an average of 8.6 percent in the 1980s and 5.5 percent in the 1990s.[3] Low interest rates, financial innovations in the primary and secondary mortgage markets, and lax oversight by Government regulators all helped spur the housing boom and the associated growth in household debt (Holt, 2009; Rampell, 2010).

The rise in housing prices was far more rapid than could be explained by increases in population and income, which are the primary determinants of demand for residential living space; housing price inflation was also driven by speculation. By the second quarter of 2006, a rising rate of loan defaults signaled that mortgage and credit card debt had reached unsustainable levels. Residential construction began to slow, average housing prices stagnated in 2006, and prices fell by 8 percent in 2007. Loan defaults accelerated over the next 2 years, precipitating the financial crisis of 2008 and the temporary near-cessation of commercial and consumer lending. By the end of 2009, median housing prices had fallen by 28 percent relative to their 2006 peak.

The collapse of the housing market had macroeconomic consequences most profoundly felt in areas that had experienced the largest housing bubbles. First came large employment losses in the building trades, where seasonally adjusted employment fell from 7.7 million in January 2007 to 5.6 million in January 2010. Second, the decline in housing prices and the sharp drop in stock values that followed reduced U.S. household wealth by an estimated $10 trillion (Rosnick and Baker, 2010). This loss of wealth has been linked to a decline in consumption as families tried to pay down their debts and rebuild their net worth, a process known as "deleveraging" (Dynan, 2012). Finally, in 2009, businesses sharply reduced their investment in structures, equipment, and software, further reducing economic output and employment.

Table 1 and figure 1 compare the depth and duration of the recession to those of the past five economic downturns, looking at the loss in nonfarm employment and the length of time before pre-recession employment levels were restored. The 2007 recession is clearly the deepest and longest lasting of those examined, and, in fact, it is the most pronounced since the Great Depression. Nonfarm employment fell by 6.3 percent (8.7 million jobs) between its peak in January 2008 and its nadir in February 2010. By comparison, peak-to-trough employment losses in the 1981 recession were half as large, at 3.1 percent.

---

[2]S&P/Case-Shiller Home Price Indices, Composite U.S. Index, and Indices for Selected Metro Areas.

[3]Department of Commerce, Bureau of Economic Analysis, National Income and Product Accounts, Table 2.1: Personal Income and Its Disposition.

Table 1
Duration and depth of past five recessions

Beginning	End	Duration (months)	Total change in nonfarm employment (percent)*	Peak monthly unemployment rate (percent)**	Time until nonfarm employment reached pre-recession peak (months)
Dec-2007	Jun-2009	18	-6.3	10.0	76
Mar-2001	Nov-2001	8	-2.0	6.3	48
Jul-1990	Mar-1991	8	-1.5	7.8	32
Jul-1981	Nov-1982	16	-3.1	10.8	28
Jan-1980	Jul-1980	6	-1.3	7.8	10

*Measured from month of highest nonfarm employment to month of lowest nonfarm employment, which may have occurred after the formal end of the recession.
**Peak unemployment associated with the recession may also occur after formal end of recession.

Source: U.S. Bureau of Labor Statistics, Current Employment Statistics (employment) and Current Population Survey (unemployment rate); National Bureau of Economic Research (recession dates).

Figure 1
Nonfarm employment trajectories during past five recessions (seasonally adjusted)

Employment index (peak = 100)

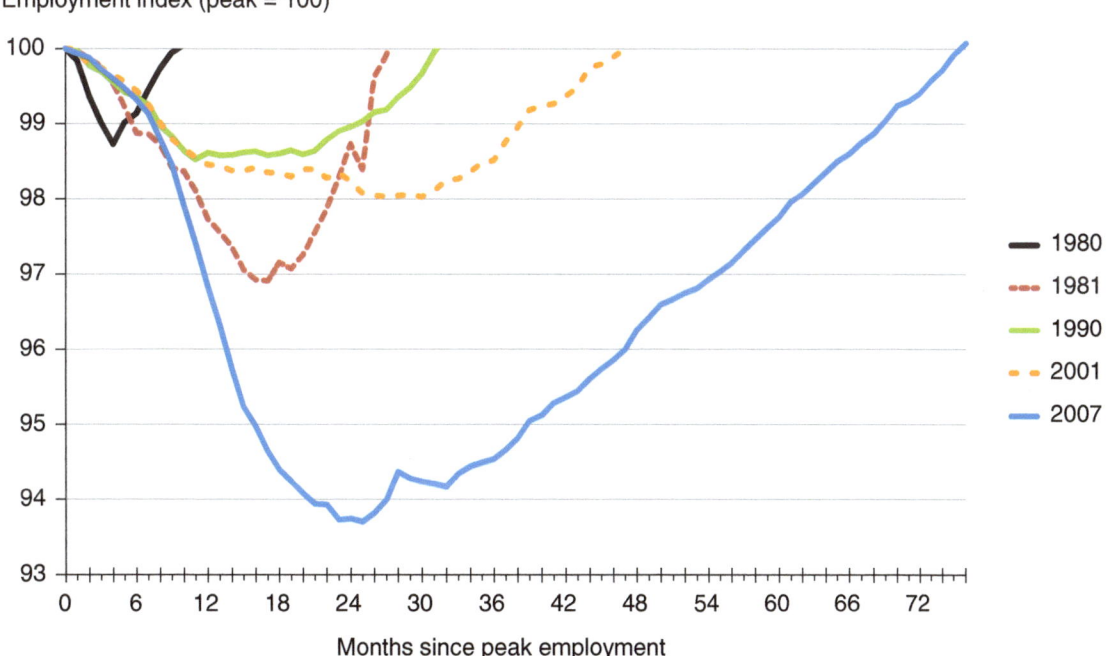

Source: U.S. Bureau of Labor Statistics, Current Employment Statistics.

The rate at which employment has rebounded following the last three recessions (which were all preceded by financial collapses) has been slower than during the recessions of 1980 and 1981 (which were the result of the Federal Reserve's efforts to curb inflation by raising interest rates, and which ended when the Federal Reserve acted to lower interest rates). Employment grew by 3 percent in the 10 months following the end of the 1981 recession, compared to less than 1 percent for the comparable interval following the 2007 recession. Employment did not match its pre-recessionary peak level until May 2014, 5 years after the end of the recession and 6.5 years after its start.

Figure 2 plots the trajectories of employment in each broad industry, beginning in January 2008. Construction was the most adversely affected, losing more than 25 percent of its employment in 2008 and 2009. Construction employment continued to fall in 2010 and has recovered very slowly since then: as of May 2014, construction employment was still 20 percent below its previous peak. Manufacturing also shed jobs rapidly, losing more than 15 percent of its employment by the end of 2009 before beginning a slow recovery; in May 2014, manufacturing employment was still 12 percent below its prior peak. By contrast, private-sector employment in education and health services has *grown* steadily for the past 6 years. Two other sectors that either avoided large employment losses during the recession or have since experienced rapid growth include farming and mining/forestry. While oil and gas production accounts for a relatively small share of national employment, its recent growth has benefited counties and States where it is concentrated, including Texas, Oklahoma, Louisiana, North Dakota, Wyoming, Kansas, Montana, and parts of Michigan, West Virginia, Pennsylvania, and Ohio.[4]

Public-sector employment held steady during the recession, in part due to support for State and local governments that was included in the American Recovery and Reinvestment Act, which has now expired. Since the end of the recession, public-sector employment has fallen by 3.1 percent,

Figure 2
Employment indices by industry

Employment index (January 2008 = 100)

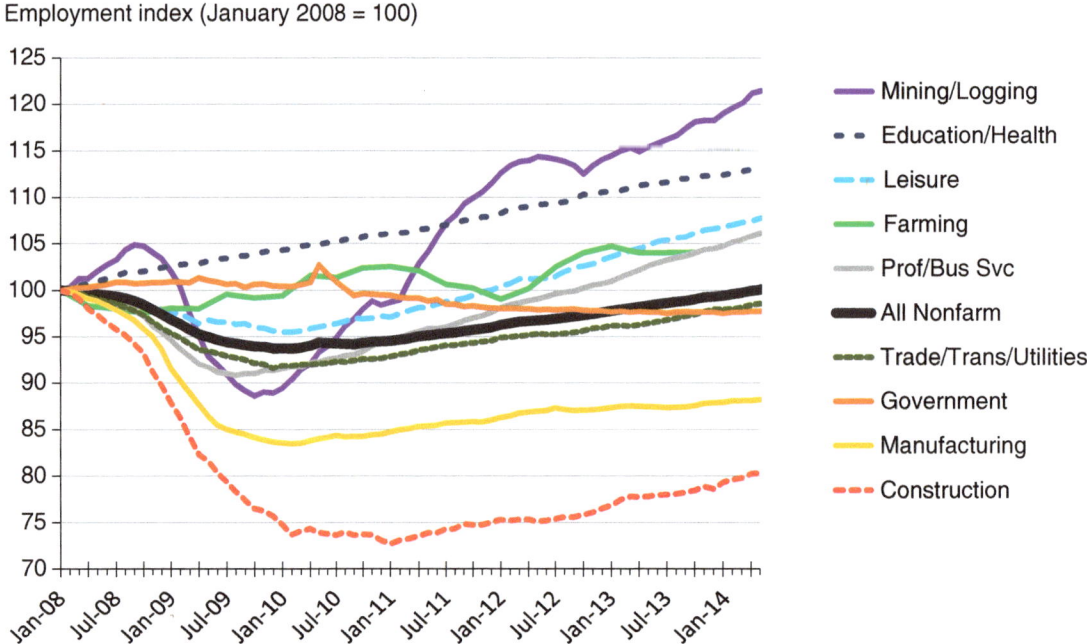

Notes: Farm employment is expressed as a rolling average of past 4 quarters to smooth seasonal fluctuations; most recent data not yet available. The spike in Government employment in April/May of 2010 reflects the temporary hiring of Census workers.
Source: U.S. Bureau of Labor Statistics, Current Employment Statistics (nonfarm employment by industry) and USDA National Agricultural Statistics Service, Farm Labor Survey (farm employment).

[4]State and county-level data on oil and gas production are available through the Economic Research Service, at: www.ers.usda.gov/data-products/county-level-oil-and-gas-production-in-the-us.

amounting to 707,000 fewer jobs in May 2014 than in June 2009 (seasonally adjusted). Fiscal pressures have forced local governments to reduce employment by some 484,000 jobs; State governments have reduced payrolls by 114,000; and another 109,000 jobs were cut by the Federal Government. This has had negative consequences for many rural counties that are highly dependent on public-sector employment. The decline in public employment has had negative multiplier effects on private-sector employment as well, and it is one of many factors contributing to the slow overall rate of employment growth. This decline is without recent precedent: government employment rose during the recoveries following the three recessions prior to the 2007-09 recession (fig. 3).

The slow rate of job growth during the recovery is all the more evident when considering the employment needs of a growing population. The employment rate (the share of the adult civilian noninstitutionalized population that is employed) has generally been rising since the 1960s, primarily due to women entering the workforce in larger numbers. On the eve of the 2007-09 recession, 63 percent of all adults, and 80 percent of prime working-age adults (ages 25-54), were employed. By 2010, both of these ratios had fallen by 5 percentage points, to levels not seen since 1983 (fig. 4). Since then, the overall employment rate has risen by just 0.4 percentage points, while the prime-age measure has risen by just 1.4 percentage points.[5] This 1-percentage-point difference implies that the aging of the workforce explains only a portion of the decline in the employment-to-population ratio since 2007. While nonfarm employment now stands at its pre-recessionary level, this rate of employment generation has been only slightly higher than the rate of growth in the adult population, which has averaged 1 percent per year since 2007.

Figure 3
Public-sector employment during last four recessions and recoveries

Employment index (start of recovery = 100)

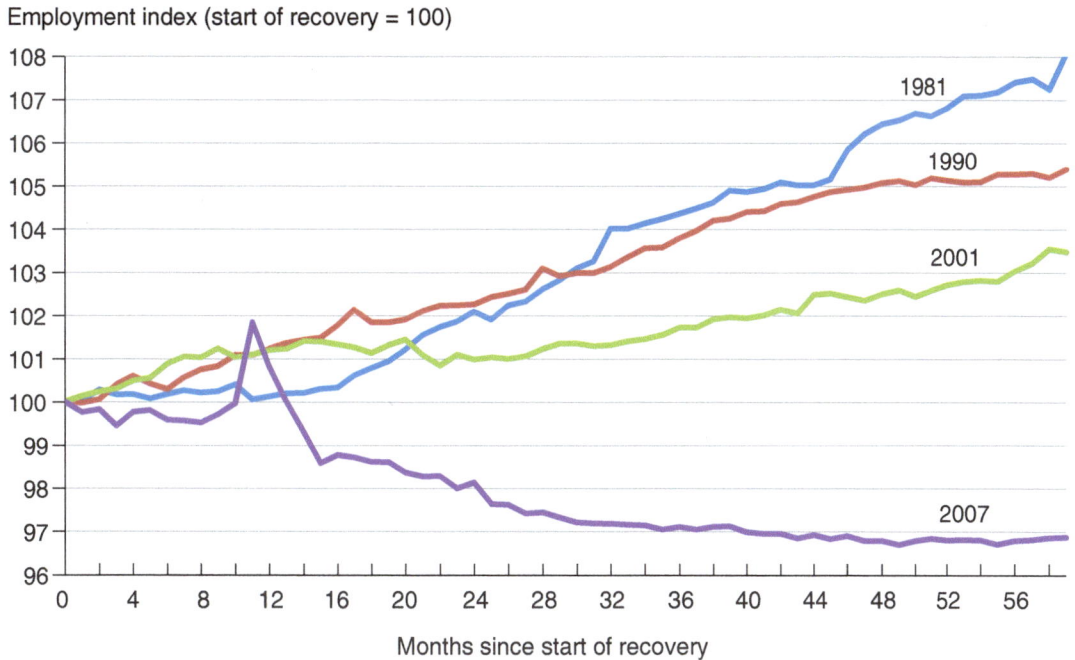

Months since start of recovery

Note: Temporary Census workers created a large temporary jump in public employment in April-May of 2010.
Source: U.S. Bureau of Labor Statistics, Current Employment Statistics.

[5]Comparing seasonally adjusted average rates for 2010 to those observed in January through May 2014.

Figure 4
Employment/population ratio (seasonally adjusted): 1962 to present

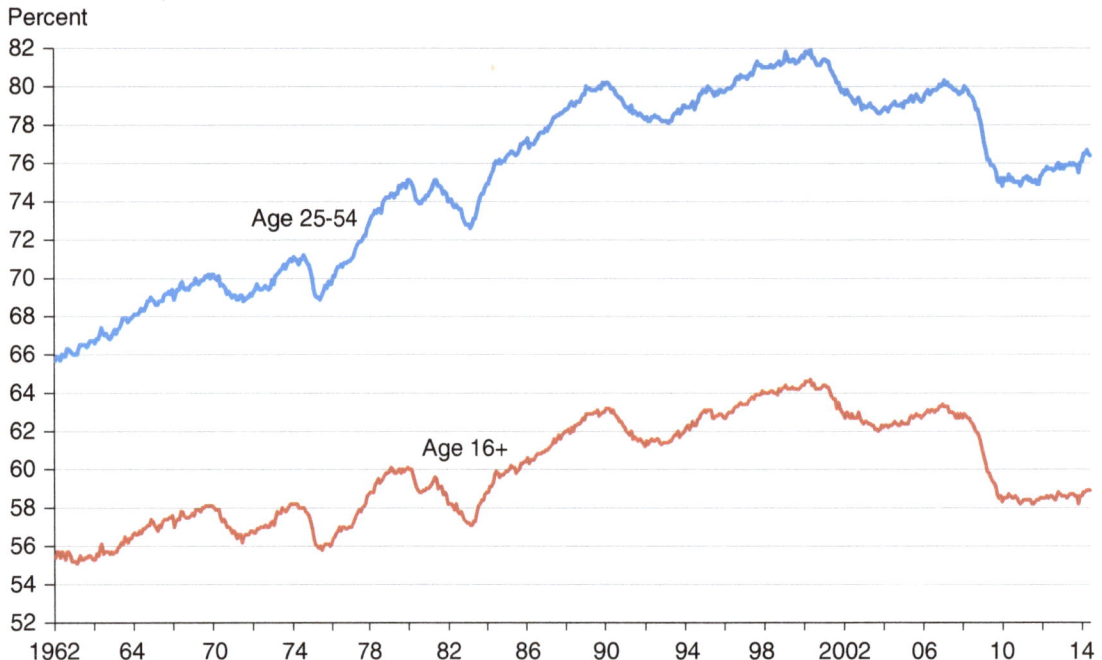

Note: The employment-population ratio measures the share of the civilian noninstitutional population in the specified age range that is employed.
Source: U.S. Bureau of Labor Statistics, Current Employment Statistics.

The labor market consequences of the recession can also be illustrated by changes in the unemployment rate. In general, employment growth and changes in county unemployment rates will move in opposite directions, but they are not simple mirror images of each other. Unlike the employment-to-population ratio, the unemployment rate takes account of the fact that the share of adults who are unable to work, or who choose not to seek work, changes over the long run, and will depend on factors such as age, education, and perceptions about employment opportunities. This has the advantage of measuring the availability of employment against the number of people who desire and are actively seeking work, rather than against the sheer number of adults. The corresponding disadvantage of the unemployment rate as a measure of labor market health, however, is that in the short run, the choice to remain outside the labor force may be influenced by the perception that no jobs are available. The unemployment rate can thus "improve" not because more people are finding jobs, but because more people are abandoning their job searches[6] or because fewer young people are choosing to enter the labor force for the first time. Indeed, this is the current state of affairs.

While the peak unemployment rate during the most recent recession (10.0 percent) was lower than the peak during the 1981 recession (10.8 percent), the pace of subsequent improvement has been slower (fig. 5). Unemployment fell by 2.5 percentage points in the 12 months following its December 1982 peak, compared to a decline of just 0.5 percentage points in the 12 months after the October 2009 peak. As of May 2014, the U.S. unemployment rate stood at 6.3 percent, 3.7 percentage points below its peak, but still 1.7 points higher than in 2007. The fact that the unemployment rate has

---

[6]People are classified as unemployed if they do not have a job, have actively looked for work at least once in the prior 4 weeks, and are currently available for work. Those who desire work but have not actively sought it are considered to be out of the labor force, rather than unemployed.

Figure 5
Monthly unemployment rate (seasonally adjusted): 1950 to present

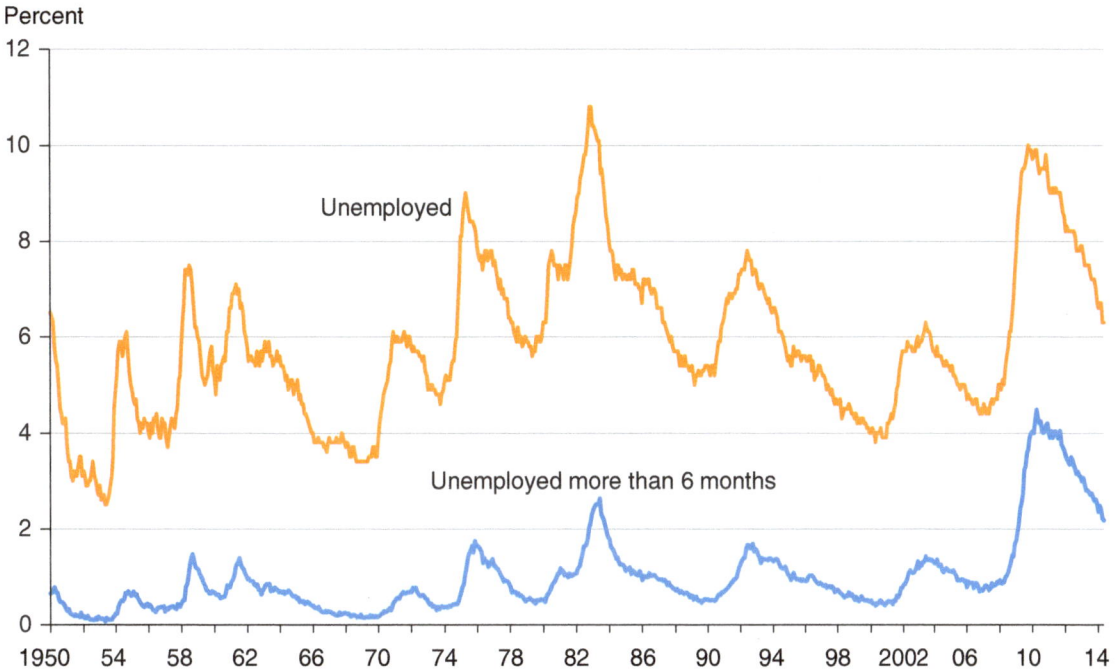

Source: U.S. Bureau of Labor Statistics, Current Employment Statistics.

improved significantly since the end of the recession, while the employment-to-population ratio has not, is testament to the many working-age adults who, for one reason or another, have given up looking for work or decided not to enter the workforce in the first place.

The depth of the recession and the slow pace of the recovery have also resulted in an unprecedented level of long-term unemployment, as measured by the share of the labor force who have been out of work for more than 6 months and are actively searching for work. This figure peaked at 4.5 percent in April 2010, the highest rate since the Great Depression, and stood at 2.2 percent in May 2014 (fig. 5, lower line).

Long-term unemployment can have longlasting effects on the income and health of unemployed workers and their families, including a negative effect on the earnings of their children as adults (Oreopoulos et al., 2008; Sullivan and Von Wachter, 2009). It can also have a negative effect on future economic growth. People who are out of work for long periods of time have been shown to suffer a deterioration in their skills, social networks, and employment prospects (Aaronson et al., 2010; Edin and Gustavsson, 2008). This depreciation of the stock of human capital implies a reduction in potential economic output and well-being (DeLong and Summers, 2012).

Regional Differences in Recession and Recovery

National trends mask important variation in regional impacts. From the fourth quarter of 2007/first quarter of 2008 through the fourth quarter of 2009/first quarter of 2010, unemployment rates rose fastest in the West, much of the South, South Atlantic, and in parts of the Midwest (fig. 6). States most reliant on manufacturing—including Michigan, Rhode Island, South Carolina, and North Carolina—were especially hard hit. Many of the States with the smallest increases in unemployment were located in the Great Plains and in the West South Central census region (which consists of Oklahoma, Texas, Louisiana, and Arkansas).

Since 2009, unemployment rates have fallen in all States, with notably large improvements in some of the harder-hit areas. In Michigan, for example, unemployment fell by 5 percentage points between the end of 2009 and the end of 2012, and stood at 7.5 percent in May 2014. This has been attributed in part to a rebound in the automobile industry, following the emergence of General Motors and Chrysler Group from their federally assisted bankruptcies in 2009. Indiana and Ohio also saw their unemployment rates fall considerably, driven in part by growth in mining, oil/gas, and related manufacturing industries (Green and Niquette, 2012).

Figure 6

Percentage point change in State unemployment rates during recession (2007Q4/2008Q1 to 2009Q4/2010Q1)

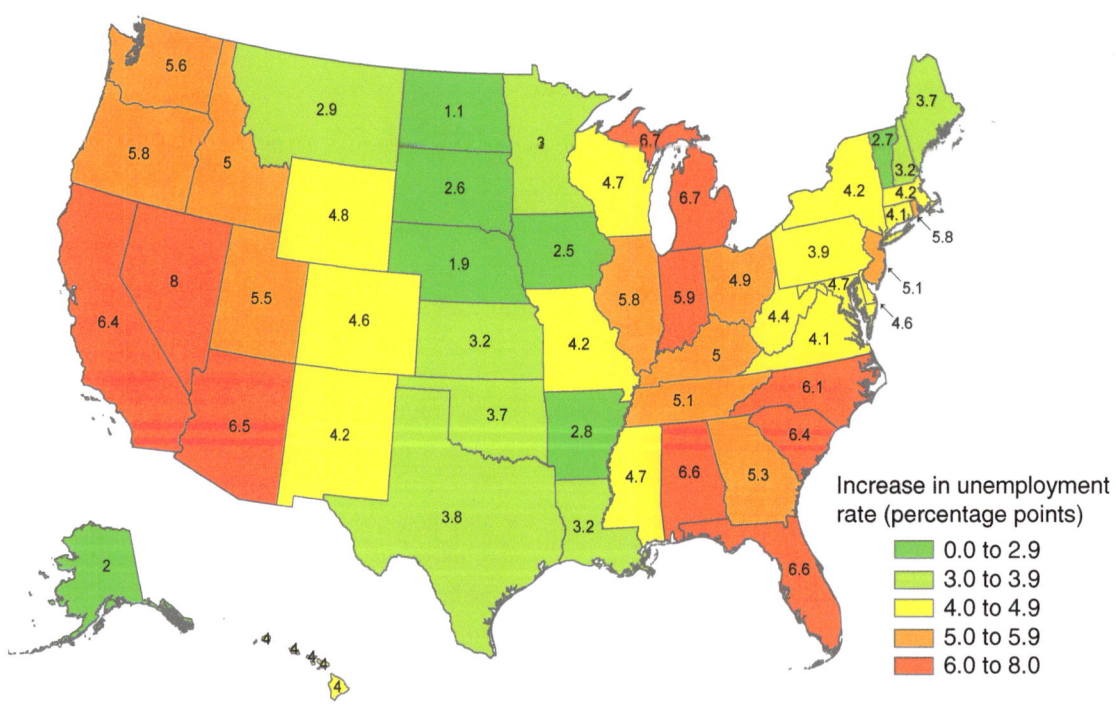

Q = Quarter. Source: USDA, Economic Research Service analysis of U.S. Bureau of Labor Statistics Local Area Unemployment data, not seasonally adjusted.

In general, States that experienced the largest increases in unemployment rates during the recession have seen the largest subsequent reductions in unemployment. Still, most of these hardest hit States remain above the national average unemployment rate. Figure 7 depicts average county-level unemployment rates for July through December of 2013 (not seasonally adjusted). The bottom quintile of counties had unemployment rates below 4.7 percent, and many of these counties are located in the Great Plains States. The highest unemployment counties (above 8.7 percent) are concentrated in the West, South, and South Atlantic, as well as in parts of the so-called Rust Belt and Appalachia.

Explaining Above-Average Employment Outcomes in the Plains States

Table 2 presents a statistical analysis to identify factors associated with disparate unemployment rate trends during the recession in counties located in the Plains States and elsewhere. In Montana, North Dakota, South Dakota, Nebraska, and Kansas, the average increase in county unemployment from the fourth quarter of 2007/first quarter of 2008 to the fourth quarter of 2009/first quarter of 2010 was 1.92 percentage points.[7] This compares to an average increase of 4.88 percentage points for counties

Figure 7
County unemployment rates, July through December 2013 (percent, not seasonally adjusted)

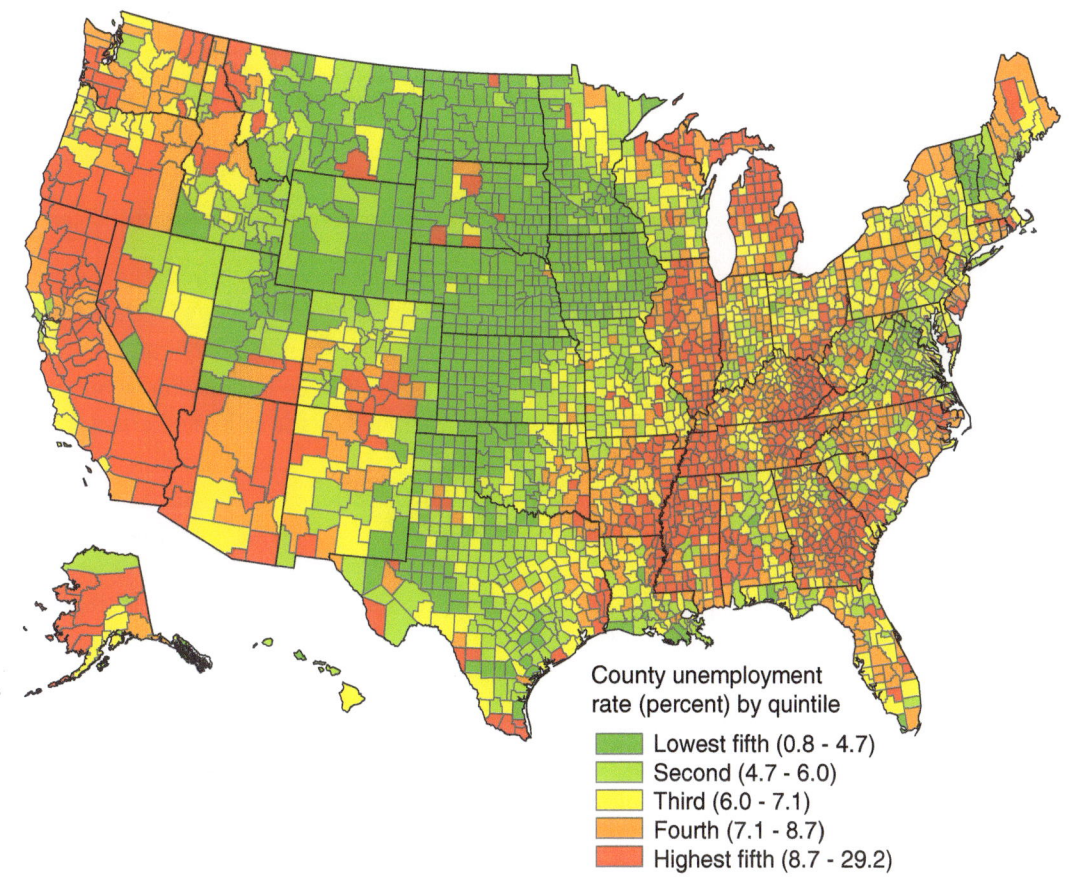

County unemployment rate (percent) by quintile

- Lowest fifth (0.8 - 4.7)
- Second (4.7 - 6.0)
- Third (6.0 - 7.1)
- Fourth (7.1 - 8.7)
- Highest fifth (8.7 - 29.2)

Source: USDA, Economic Research Service analysis of U.S. Bureau of Labor Statistics Local Area Unemployment data, not seasonally adjusted.

---

[7]We work with unweighted averages of county-level labor market statistics in this and subsequent statistical analyses. These unweighted county averages differ from the statewide results in figure 6 because the latter implicitly assign more weight to larger counties. The advantage of placing equal weight on counties of all sizes is that the experiences of smaller more rural counties are not obscured by the outcomes in larger counties. Our unweighted results may be thought of as pertaining to an average or representative county rather than the county in which the average or representative person lives.

Table 2

Factors associated with smaller increase in unemployment in five Plains States during recession

	Change in unemployment rate (percentage points)	
Counties in ND, SD, NE, MT, and KS	1.92	
Rest of country	4.88	
Difference	-2.96	‡
Explained by differences in attributes	-1.42	‡
Unexplained	-1.54	‡
Contributions of attributes		
Industrial composition	-0.93	‡
Educational composition	-0.28	‡
Age distribution	-0.10	
Population growth in prior period	-0.10	†
Sample size	3130	
R^2 (pooled model)	0.40	

† Statistically significant at p < 0.10; ‡ statistically significant at p < 0.05.
Note: Recession period defined as running from the 4th quarter of 2007/1st quarter of 2008 to the 4th quarter of 2009/1st quarter of 2010. Seven small nonmetro counties with unrealistically large estimated employment growth rates during the recovery are dropped for consistency with later analyses; these likely reflect imperfections in the LAUS county employment estimation methodology.

Source: USDA, ERS analysis of Local Area Unemployment Statistics employment data; see Appendix for description of methods and details of variable definitions and data sources.

in the other 45 States. The difference of 2.96 percentage points is statistically significant, and we seek to explain this gap with regression equations that model the changes in county unemployment rates as a function of the attributes listed in the lower panel of Table 2. (Details on variable definitions and the regression specification are provided in the Appendix.) Differences between the five Plains States and the rest of the country in the average level of each attribute, multiplied by the estimated effect of that attribute on the unemployment rate, yield estimates of the contribution of each attribute to the overall unemployment rate gap. The model found that roughly half (1.42 percentage points) of the gap in unemployment rate increases can be explained by the variables that are included in the model.

The contribution of each explanatory variable is reported in the second panel of Table 2; the entries sum, within rounding error, to the explained total (-1.42 percentage points). The Plains States' favorable mix of industries at the start of the recession served to moderate the recession-induced increase in unemployment by an estimated 0.93 percentage points. In particular, Plains counties were far more likely to have farming-dependent economies, as defined by the Economic Research Service's county typology system,[8] and this reduced unemployment rates by 0.34 percentage points as compared to non-Plains counties (detail not reported in table). Equally important, however, were the Plains counties' much _lower_ shares of employment in the rapidly contracting manufacturing

---

[8]The ERS County Typology system uses both public and restricted-access county-level data from the Census Bureau and the Bureau of Economic Analysis to classify all U.S. counties according to six non-overlapping categories of economic dependence. The codes and their definitions are available at: www.ers.usda.gov/data-products/county-typology-codes.aspx.

sector, which reduced their unemployment rates by another 0.37 percentage points relative to non-Plains counties. Plains counties also had a lower-than-average share of employment in professional services, which shrank rapidly during the recession, and this reduced their 2009 end-of-year unemployment rate by another 0.14 percentage points (details not reported in table).

The model found a significant negative relationship between local unemployment rates and the share of the adult population that were college graduates. This college-educated share was higher in the average county in the Plains States (52 percent, including both those with some college education and 4-year-college graduates) than in non-Plains counties (46 percent, details not reported in table). During the recession, their higher levels of education served to limit the increase in unemployment in Plains counties, reducing it by an estimated 0.28 percentage points compared to counties in non-Plains States.

The final significant factor identified by the model was the rate of population growth, measured over the year prior to the recession so as to not reflect the effects of the recession itself. Differences between county population growth rates largely reflect a longstanding pattern of lower population growth in more rural areas, and this slower rate of growth in the size of the labor force will mechanically reduce unemployment rates for any given rate of job creation. According to these estimates, lower population growth reduced unemployment rates in the Plains States by 0.10 percentage points, on average, compared to what they would have experienced had their population growth rates been more similar to those observed in the remaining 45 States.

To summarize, the smaller increase in county unemployment rates in the five Plains States examined here was partly a result of a more favorable mix of industries, one that was skewed toward agriculture and away from manufacturing and professional services. Higher educational attainment and lower population growth also contributed to limiting the increase in unemployment rates during the recession. However, about half of the Plains States' unemployment rate advantage (1.54 percentage points) cannot be explained by the variables in the model. The most likely reason for this is that our county-level data on industrial employment shares are coded in fairly broad categories and cannot fully capture the finer differences in industrial composition between counties in Plains and non-Plains States.

Recession and Recovery in Rural and Urban Counties

The degree of rurality was another important geographic determinant of employment and unemployment rates. We explore urban/rural differences in employment outcomes, using metropolitan/nonmetropolitan county status as our definition of the urban/rural divide, following the 2013 U.S. Office of Management and Budget (OMB) metropolitan definition in all years.

Metro and Nonmetro Employment Trends Have Diverged During the Recovery

Figure 8 plots seasonally adjusted quarterly indices of the number of employed people living in metro and nonmetro counties, with the first quarter of 2007 as the base period (at an index value of 100). The data come from the Bureau of Labor Statistics' Local Area Unemployment Statistics (LAUS) program, which counts full- and part-time wage and salary workers as well as the self-employed, thus capturing many small business owners who are omitted from counts of wage and salary employment alone. Employment is based on the worker's place of residence, not on their place of employment.[9]

Figure 8
Nonmetro and metro quarterly employment indices, 2007 to present (seasonally adjusted)

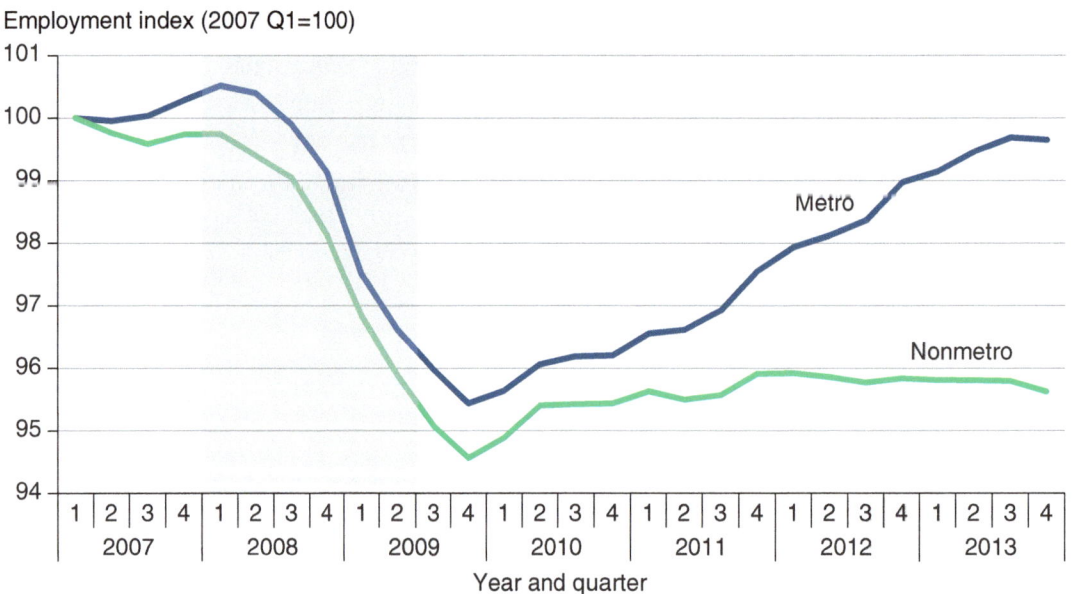

Notes: Shaded area indicates recession period, as determined by National Bureau of Economic Research. Metro/nonmetro classification follows the 2013 U.S. Office of Management and Budget (OMB) categories in all years. New population controls were introduced into the LAUS data following the April 2010 Census, leading to an increase in estimated employment in the second quarter of 2010. The data shown have been corrected to compensate for this change, but the correction is approximate and caution should be used in comparing employment levels before and after this date. The scale of the vertical axis was chosen to emphasize short-run variation during and after the 2007 recession. Source: U.S. Bureau of Labor Statistics, Local Area Unemployment Statistics (LAUS, seasonally adjusted by ERS).

---

[9]The LAUS employment and unemployment definitions are consistent with the Current Population Survey (CPS), and contemporaneous State-level estimates from the LAUS are constrained to agree with CPS. However, metro/nonmetro totals in the LAUS are not controlled to match CPS results. We rely on the LAUS estimates, adjusted as described in the notes to fig. 8, and aggregated to conform to the 2013 OMB metro definition, which cannot be replicated in CPS public-use microdata files.

Employment of nonmetro residents peaked in the first quarter of 2007 and had begun to fall *prior* to the official onset of the recession in December 2007. This pattern is unusual—nonmetro areas usually lag rather than lead national employment trends. By the end of 2009, nonmetro employment had fallen by 5.4 percent. Metro employment, by contrast, grew during 2007 and peaked in the first quarter of 2008, a full year after the nonmetro peak. Metro employment then fell for the next 2 years, and by the end of 2009, it was 5 percent below its peak value (fig. 8). Estimated employment losses as a proportion of their peak value thus appear slightly larger (but by just 0.4 percentage points) in nonmetro than metro areas and began a year earlier.

Employment recovered over the course of 2010, growing at a comparable pace in metro and nonmetro counties. But nonmetro employment growth slowed in 2011, and fell to zero or slightly below thereafter; total nonmetro employment was estimated at 20,165,000 in the fourth quarter of 2013, compared to 20,224,000 in the fourth quarter of 2011. As a result, the gap between the metro and nonmetro employment indices has grown rapidly in the past 3 years.

Explaining Slow Employment Growth in Nonmetro Counties During the Recovery

Table 3 uses the same statistical approach described above to examine the factors associated with the slower pace of the recovery in nonmetro areas. The recovery is defined as the 4-year interval starting in the fourth quarter of 2009/first quarter of 2010 and running until the fourth quarter of 2013/ first quarter of 2014.[10] Although the underlying data are not seasonally adjusted, the comparison of the same quarters in each period mitigates the effects of seasonality. As before, we work with unweighted averages of county-level labor market statistics, so that the results are not dominated by the experience of the most populous and least rural counties.[11]

Over the 4-year recovery period, employment grew by 1.57 percent (cumulatively, not annually) in the average nonmetro county, compared to 3.82 percent in the average metro county (table 3). The difference (2.25 percentage points) is statistically significant, and the model manages to explain more than two-thirds of this gap (1.56 percentage points) using the variables listed in the second panel of table 3. These are the same county-level attributes as in the Plains States analysis in table 2, with the addition of a set of dummy variables that identify the 50 States. The inclusion of these State effects implies that we are estimating the effect of each variable on differences between metro and nonmetro counties *within* each State.

The contribution of each explanatory variable is reported in the second panel of the table; the entries again sum to the explained total, with negative numbers indicating factors that worked against nonmetro areas. Among the variables considered, the most important was the lower prior rate of population growth in nonmetro areas, which accounted for 1.14 percentage points of the nonmetro employment growth deficit. In other words, slower population growth in rural areas can account

---

[10]Employment growth results for the recovery period are not corrected for the change in population controls in the LAUS data introduced in the second quarter of 2010; this implies that the percentage increase in employment during this period is slightly overstated for all county types, but comparisons between county types are likely only marginally affected.

[11]We drop seven small nonmetro counties whose employment levels grew by more than 50 percent over this time period. These exceptionally high growth rates are most likely artifacts of the methods LAUS uses to allocate employment across counties.

Table 3

Factors associated with slower employment growth during the recovery in nonmetro counties

	Change in employment rate (percent)
Nonmetro	1.57
Metro	3.82
Difference	-2.25 ‡
Explained by differences in attributes	-1.56 ‡
Unexplained	-0.68 ‡
Contributions of attributes	
State effects	0.18
Industrial composition	0.57 †
Educational composition	-0.73 ‡
Age distribution	-0.39 ‡
Population growth in prior period	-1.14 ‡
Employment growth in prior period	-0.05
Sample size	3130
R^2 (pooled model)	0.27

†Statistically significant at $p < 0.10$; ‡statistically significant at $p < 0.05$.

Note: Recovery period defined as running from the 4th quarter of 2009/1st quarter of 2010 to the 4th quarter of 2013/1st quarter of 2014. Seven small nonmetro counties with unrealistically large estimated employment growth rates during the recovery are dropped; these likely reflect imperfections in the LAUS county employment estimation methodology.

Source: USDA, ERS analysis of Local Area Unemployment Statistics employment data; see Appendix for description of methods and details of variable definitions and data sources.

for half (1.14 out of 2.25 percentage points) of their slower rate of job growth as compared to metro areas. (See also table 4 for more information on metro/nonmetro population growth rates.)

Consistent with previous research (e.g., Gottlieb and Fogarty, 2003), a significant positive relationship was found between local employment growth rates and the share of the adult population that were college graduates. This college-educated share was lower in nonmetro counties (16 percent) than in metro areas (23 percent, numbers not reported in table), and this gap reduced nonmetro employment growth relative to growth in metro areas during the recovery. Taken together, metro/nonmetro differences in attainment across all educational levels account for 0.73 percentage points of the recent deficit in nonmetro job growth, about one-third of the total.

Differences between the metro and nonmetro age structures accounted for another 0.39 percentage points of the metro/nonmetro job growth gap. This was due to a negative relationship between job growth and the share of the population that was 55 and older, particularly the share in the near-retirement age category of 55-64. Both shares were higher in nonmetro counties.

Differences in industrial composition appear to slightly favor nonmetro areas within each State, adding 0.57 percentage points to cumulative employment growth relative to metro counties since the end of the recession. About half of this effect is due to nonmetro areas' higher employment shares in the relatively prosperous agriculture and mining industries.

To summarize, the slower rate of population growth in nonmetro areas can explain half of their employment growth deficit during the 2010-13 recovery. Employers also appear to be creating more jobs in areas that have younger and better educated workforces, all else being equal, and both of these factors work against nonmetro areas. These findings are based on measuring population growth, age structure, and educational attainment in the years prior to the recovery. This mitigates the concern about "reverse causality" and supports the conclusion that the employment trends are effects, not causes, of population growth, education, and age differences although our model only identifies statistical relationships; it cannot explicitly test for causality. Together, these effects outweighed the benefits of a more favorable mix of industries, in particular a higher employment share in agricultural and extractive industries.

Population Growth Has Slowed to Near Zero in Nonmetro Counties

Except for the 1970s, population growth has historically been more rapid in metro than in nonmetro counties. The estimated growth rate of the adult (age 16 and older) civilian noninstitutionalized population (CNP)[12] has recently slowed. In urban areas, it fell from 1.26 percent per year for 2007 to 2008 to 0.85 percent for 2012-13 (table 4). In nonmetro areas, population growth has declined more markedly, falling from 0.49 percent per year in 2008 to 0.19 percent in 2011, and reaching -0.07 percent in 2013. This is thought to be the first time that the nonmetro population has declined in absolute levels from one year to the next. [13]

Table 4

Estimates of civilian noninstitutionalized adult population (ages 16 and above) in metro and nonmetro areas, 2007-2013

	2007	2008	2009	2010	2011	2012	2013
Metro							
Population (millions)	196.9	199.3	201.7	203.9	206.2	208.6	210.3
Annual growth (percent)		1.26	1.21	1.08	1.12	1.14	0.85
Nonmetro							
Population (millions)	35.34	35.51	35.64	35.77	35.84	35.86	35.84
Annual growth (percent)		0.49	0.36	0.37	0.19	0.07	-0.07
Total							
Population (millions)	232.2	234.9	237.4	239.7	242.1	244.4	246.2
Annual growth (percent)		1.14	1.08	0.98	0.98	0.98	0.72

Note: Metro/nonmetro classification follows the 2013 U.S. Office of Management and Budget (OMB) categories in all years. Underlying population estimates as of July 1 of each year.

Source: USDA, ERS analysis of data from U.S. Census Bureau.

[12]The CNP consists of persons 16 years of age and older who are not living in institutions such as prisons, hospitals, or homes for the aged, and who are not on active duty in the Armed Forces.

[13]See "Population & Migration" on the ERS website, at www.ers.usda.gov/topics/rural-economy-population/population-migration.aspx, for more information.

This leveling off of the nonmetro population represents the joint effect of two trends: a continued longrun decline in the rate of natural population increase in nonmetro areas (due to declining nonmetro birth rates and rising death rates as the nonmetro population ages) and a recent decline in net migration to nonmetro areas, which peaked in 2006, then fell sharply, and has been negative (indicating net outmigration) since 2010. The shift to net outmigration from rural areas is likely a consequence of nonmetro employment losses associated with the recession. Whereas suburban expansion and migration to scenic, retirement, and recreation-oriented destinations have historically been the primary drivers of rural demographic change, the influence of these factors has weakened since the recession, while the importance of job losses in manufacturing and other hard-hit economic sectors has increased.

Both Metro and Nonmetro Employment-to-Population Ratios Have Been Flat Since 2010

The nonmetro population is older and has a larger share of retired workers than is found in metro counties; as a result, nonmetro employment-to-population ratios are lower (fig. 9). Although these areas lost a comparable or even slightly greater share of employment during the recession than did metro counties, their much slower population growth meant that their average employment-to-population ratio declined *less* rapidly than for urban areas. The nonmetro employment-to-population ratio fell by 4.0 percentage points between the first quarter of 2007 and the fourth quarter of 2009, compared to a decline of 4.9 percentage points for metro areas.[14] Since 2010, the share of the population that is employed has remained effectively constant in both metro and nonmetro areas, meaning that their job growth rates have more or less exactly matched their respective population growth rates. Current employment rates are the lowest observed in the past 30 years (see also fig. 4).

Recent Declines in Metro and Nonmetro Unemployment Rates Are Due to Reduced Labor Force Participation

Unlike the employment-to-population ratios, the unemployment rate has recovered significantly since the end of the recession. In 2007, the nonmetro unemployment rate averaged 5.1 percent, compared to 4.5 percent in urban areas (fig. 10). As the recession unfolded, however, metro and nonmetro unemployment rates rose rapidly and converged, peaking at 10.1 percent in the fourth quarter of 2009 in nonmetro counties, and at 9.9 percent in the first quarter of 2010 in metro areas. Since that time, the two unemployment rates have followed very similar downward trends. The seasonally adjusted nonmetro unemployment rate stood at 7.2 percent in the fourth quarter of 2013, compared to 6.9 percent for metro areas. The fact that unemployment rates are falling, but employment rates are not rising, is an indication that a smaller share of the adult population is seeking employment—in other words, labor force participation is falling. In both metro and nonmetro areas, employment growth has matched population growth. Declines in the unemployment rate are thus entirely due to decreases in the number of people looking for work, not an increase in the share of the population that is working.

---

[14]The Bureau of Labor Statistics does not report employment-to-population ratios for metro versus nonmetro areas. The figures reported here were calculated by aggregating the LAUS county employment estimates into metro and nonmetro totals, adjusting for changes in population weights (see notes to fig. 8), and dividing by our own estimates of the civilian noninstitutionalized population for metro and nonmetro areas. These latter start with the Census Bureau's inter- and post-censal estimates of the adult population, by county, and adjust for estimated shares residing on military bases and in institutions such as prisons and nursing homes, using detailed county population data from the 2010 Census. When aggregated to the national level, the metro and nonmetro employment-to-population estimates reported here agree with the official CPS-based estimates plotted in fig. 4 to within two-tenths of a percentage point.

Figure 9
Nonmetro versus metro employment/population ratio (seasonally adjusted)

Percent of adults employed

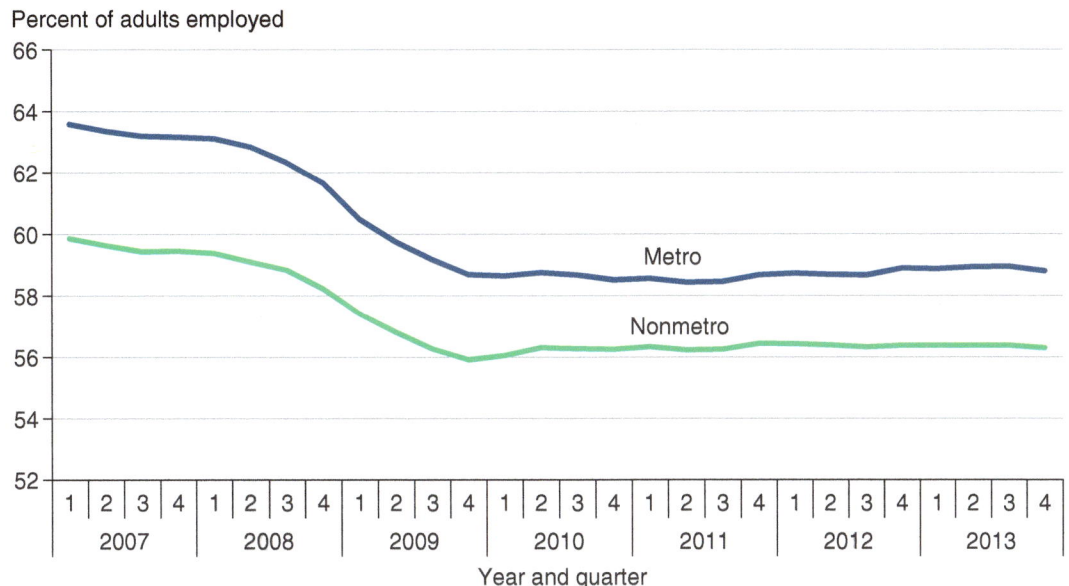

Notes: Employed people as percentage of estimated adult (16 and older) civilian noninstitutionalized population.
Metro/nonmetro classification follows the 2013 U.S. Office of Management and Budget (OMB) categories in all years.
See notes to fig. 8 concerning break in data series in the second quarter of 2010. The scale of the vertical axis was
chosen to emphasize short-run variation during and after the 2007 recession.
Source: USDA, Economic Research Service analysis of data from Bureau of Labor Statistics, Local Area Unemployment
Statistics, and U.S. Census Bureau.

Figure 10
Nonmetro versus metro quarterly unemployment rates (seasonally adjusted)

Unemployment rate (percent)

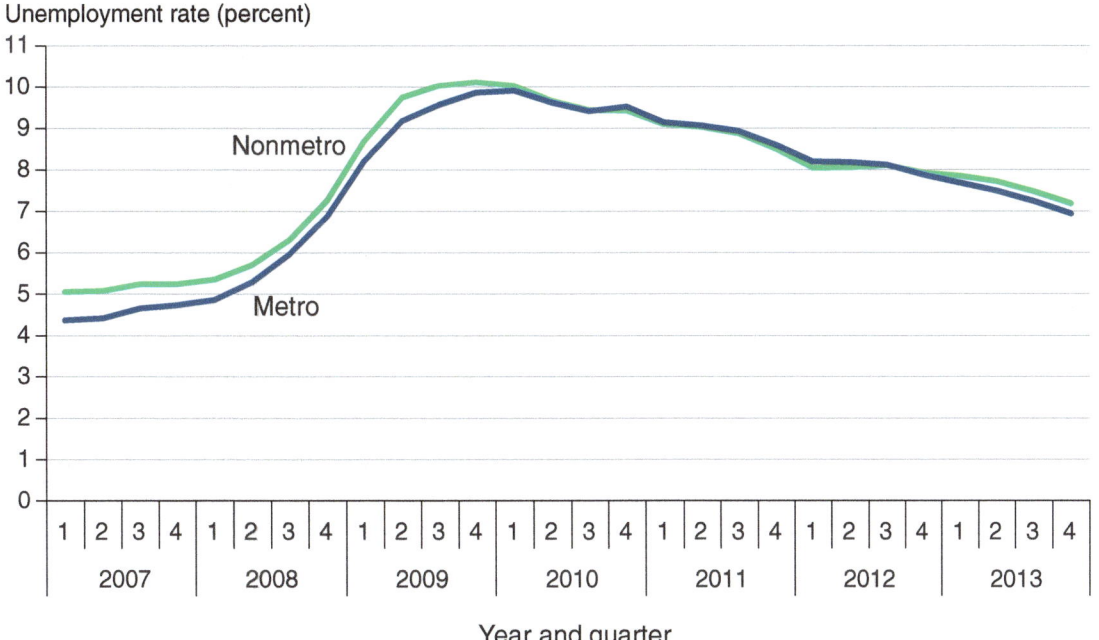

Note: Metro/nonmetro classification follows the 2013 U.S. Office of Management and Budget (OMB) categories in all
years. Source: U.S. Bureau of Labor Statistics, Local Area Unemployment Statistics, seasonally adjusted by USDA,
Economic Research Service.

Variation in Labor Market Outcomes Among Nonmetro Counties

We now examine which types of rural counties were most affected by the recession, and why. We focus on some of the largest observed differences in outcomes between counties of various geographic, economic and social types. The factors we consider are detailed in table 5 and reflect previous findings in the literature. Taking county characteristics into account, we look at employment outcome differences among counties categorized by population density, adjacency to metro areas, and racial and ethnic makeup, all of which were among the most powerful predictors of employment and unemployment growth during the recession and in the recovery. The most sparsely populated nonmetro counties fared best in terms of employment and unemployment rates, as did counties that were not adjacent to metro areas. Counties with large Hispanic population shares also fared relatively well in terms of employment outcomes, whereas counties with large African-American population shares have displayed subpar employment outcomes during both the recession and the recovery. As before, we define the recession period to run from the fourth quarter of 2007/ first quarter of 2008 through the fourth quarter of 2009/first quarter of 2010. The recovery period includes the subsequent 4 years, ending in the fourth quarter of 2013/first quarter of 2014.

The Least Densely Populated Rural Counties Experienced Smaller Job Losses

For counties in the lowest population-density category,[15] average employment fell by just 1.3 percent during the recession, compared to 5-6 percent for medium- and high-density nonmetro counties (table 5). The reasons for this difference are explored in column 1 of table 6, which groups medium- and high-density counties together for clarity. The 4.42 percentage points that separate the employment loss rates in the two types of counties were fully explained by the variables in the model. The largest contribution, accounting for 3.33 percentage points of additional employment in low-density counties, comes from State location effects. Low-population-density counties are disproportionately located in States in the Northern Plains and Mountain regions, where employment in both low- and higher density counties was less affected by the recession. Low-density counties also benefited from a favorable mix of industries, having much lower shares of manufacturing employment, higher shares of farm employment, and somewhat higher shares of Federal employment. Together, these industrial composition effects raised employment growth (or reduced employment losses) by 1.86 percentage points relative to more densely populated nonmetro areas. None of the other variables considered, such as age and education distributions, were significant in explaining the better employment outcomes in low-density counties.

Employment growth appears to have been slightly more rapid in low-density nonmetro counties during the 4 years of recovery (table 6, column 2), although the 1.06 percentage point difference between low and higher density counties was not statistically different from zero. None of the factors explaining differences in employment growth rates during the recession appear to have extended their influence into the recovery phase to any statistically significant degree. This lack of influence is also reflected in the lower R-squared value associated with this regression: whereas 54 percent of the variance in employment growth rates across nonmetro counties can be explained by the model

---

[15]The lowest density counties had an unweighted average population density of 5.8 people per square mile, while the middle group averaged 27 people per square mile, and the most densely populated third of nonmetro counties averaged 95 people per square mile. By comparison, metro counties had an average population density of 606 people per square mile.

Table 5
Nonmetro county employment and unemployment in recession and recovery

	Change in employment (percent)		Change in unemployment rate (percentage points)	
	Recession	Recovery	Recession	Recovery
Population density category				
Low density	-1.3	2.3	3.1	-1.8
Medium density	-5.2	1.1	4.7	-2.8
High density	-6.2	1.4	5.4	-3.4
Adjacency status				
Not adjacent to metro area	-3.2	1.4	3.8	-2.2
Adjacent to small metro	-5.0	1.5	4.8	-3.0
Adjacent to large metro	-5.7	2.3	5.3	-3.6
Racial/ethnic composition				
>25% African American	-7.9	-1.4	5.9	-3.4
>25% Hispanic	0.2	4.6	3.9	-2.1
>25% Native American	-1.4	0.6	3.1	-0.5
No large minority populations	-4.1	1.8	4.2	-2.7
All nonmetro counties	-4.2	1.6	4.4	-2.7

Notes: Recession period runs from 2007Q4/2008Q1 to 2009Q4/2010Q1. Recovery period runs through 2013Q4/2014Q1. Sample limited to 1,964 nonmetro counties, as designated by the 2013 U.S. Office of Management and Budget (OMB). Seven small nonmetro counties with unrealistically large estimated employment growth rates during the recovery are dropped; these likely reflect imperfections in the LAUS county employment estimation methodology. These are un-weighted county averages of percentage changes in employment and percentage point changes in the unemployment rate. See Appendix for explanation of regression methods and variable definitions.

Source: USDA, ERS analysis of Local Area Unemployment Statistics data, not seasonally adjusted.

during the recession, only 23 percent of that variance is explained during the recovery. In other words, patterns of employment change among nonmetro counties have been less predictable during the recovery than they were during the recession. However, there is evidence that counties that lost larger shares of employment during the recession are regaining employment more rapidly during the recovery, which is helping the medium- and high-density nonmetro counties.

The observed increase in unemployment rates during the recession was 1.98 percentage points smaller in low-density counties than in medium- and high-density areas, and virtually all of this difference can be explained by the county attributes listed (table 6, column 3). As with employment growth, much of the low-density-county advantage relates to their State locations (resulting in 0.74 percentage points less unemployment) and more favorable industrial mix (0.62 percentage points). However, other significant factors emerge as well. In particular, lower density counties have a slightly higher share of college-educated workers, including those with some college education but not a 4-year degree, and this was associated with a slight reduction in the unemployment rate (0.11 percentage points) relative to higher density counties. Slower population growth (measured in the prior period) also made a modest contribution to reducing the unemployment rate in low-density counties (by 0.06 percentage points).

The final variable listed in the table is a measure of the county unemployment rate at the start of the period. This variable captures the short-run dynamic behavior of the unemployment rate, or the

Table 6

Factors associated with better employment outcomes in low-population-density nonmetro counties

	Change in employment (percent)		Change in unemployment rate (percentage points)	
	Recession	Recovery	Recession	Recovery
Low population density counties	-1.27	2.28	3.06	-1.79
Medium or high density counties	-5.69	1.22	5.04	-3.14
Difference	4.42 ‡	1.06	-1.98 ‡	1.35 ‡
Explained by differences in attributes	4.85 ‡	1.61 ‡	-1.86 ‡	1.42 ‡
Unexplained	-0.44	-0.55	-0.13	-0.07
Contributions of attributes				
State effects	3.33 ‡	1.36	-0.74 ‡	0.11
Industrial composition	1.86 ‡	0.48	-0.62 ‡	0.35 ‡
Educational Composition	-0.19	0.48	-0.11 ‡	-0.19 †
Age distribution	0.02	-0.21	0.00	-0.01
Population growth in prior period	-0.07	0.06	-0.06 †	0.00
Outcome in prior period*	-0.10	-0.56 ‡	-0.32 ‡	1.17 ‡
Sample size	1964	1964	1964	1964
R^2 (pooled model)	0.54	0.23	0.69	0.65

† Statistically significant at $p < 0.10$; ‡ statistically significant at $p < 0.05$.

* In the employment change regressions, this variable is equal to the percent employment change in the prior 2-year period. In the unemployment change regressions, it is equal to the unemployment level at the start of the period.

Notes: Recession period runs from 2007Q4/2008Q1 to 2009Q4/2010Q1. Recovery period runs through 2013Q4/2014Q1. Sample limited to 1,964 nonmetro counties, as designated by the 2013 Office of Management and Budget (OMB). Seven small nonmetro counties with unrealistically large estimated employment growth rates during the recovery are dropped; these likely reflect imperfections in the LAUS county employment estimation methodology. See Appendix for explanation of regression methods and variable definitions.

Source: USDA, ERS analysis of Local Area Unemployment Statistics data, not seasonally adjusted.

degree to which unemployment rate movements are influenced by the initial level of unemployment in any given period. In the recession, these effects were positive: unemployment rate increases were larger in counties that had higher initial unemployment rates, resulting in a widening of the gap between high- and low-unemployment counties. To determine how this influenced the relative performance of low-density versus higher density nonmetro counties, we note that low-density counties had a lower average unemployment rate at the onset of the recession; as a result, they experienced somewhat smaller average increases in unemployment than did the higher density counties, as indicated by the negative coefficient (-0.32 percentage points).

During the recovery period, however, these dynamics were reversed. Counties with higher post-recession unemployment rates tended to experience greater subsequent *reductions* in unemployment. This process, known as reversion to the mean, is working to reduce the gap between high- and low-unemployment counties. Since the higher-population-density counties were at higher levels of unemployment when the recovery began, they experienced considerably larger subsequent declines. Indeed, the coefficient on the variable labeled "Outcome in Prior Period" in the final column of table 6 (1.17 percentage points) demonstrates that reversion to the mean can account for the bulk of the gap between unemployment rate reductions experienced by low-density counties (where unemployment has fallen by 1.79 percent) and higher density counties (where it has fallen by 3.14 percent).

To summarize, the smaller job losses experienced during the recession by the most rural, least densely populated counties relative to more densely populated (but still nonmetro) counties appear largely to reflect State- and county-level differences in economic structure and industrial mix, with differences in manufacturing, mining, and Federal employment shares looming largest. These same factors also explain their smaller increases in unemployment, with additional contributions coming from a slightly more favorable educational composition and slower population growth. Dynamic effects, whereby lower initial unemployment rates were associated with lower subsequent increases in unemployment rates, also favored the lower-population-density counties during the recession. During the recovery, however, these dynamic effects reversed sign, and higher unemployment counties reduced their unemployment rates faster. This has narrowed the gap between the unemployment rates of high- and low-density nonmetro counties, but it remains true that the net increase in unemployment over the course of the recession and recovery has been smallest in low-population-density counties.

Counties Adjacent to Metro Areas Lost Employment More Rapidly

Employment losses during the recession were greatest in nonmetro counties that were adjacent to small or large metro areas (table 5, panel 2). These counties lost 5.0 to 5.7 percent of their employment, while nonadjacent counties lost 3.2 percent. Nonadjacent counties also experienced smaller increases in unemployment rates during the recession (3.8 percentage points versus 4.8 to 5.3 percentage points for adjacent counties).

The gap between adjacent and nonadjacent counties in the rate of employment loss was driven by many of the same factors that explain the differences between low- and medium-/high-density counties, namely, the effects of State location and industrial composition (table 7, column 1).[16] Differences in the share of employment in manufacturing were again most important. Prior to the recession, the share of employment in manufacturing was 15.5 percent in counties adjacent to metro areas, versus 9.9 percent in nonadjacent counties. This greater exposure to the rapidly contracting manufacturing sector was associated with 0.61 percentage points of additional job loss in adjacent counties (number not shown in table). Adjacent counties were also disadvantaged by their lower shares of Federal employment and by a smaller share of employment in agriculture and mining; together, these aspects of their industry mix reduced employment by another 0.28 percentage points (not shown in table). Taken together, the effects of industrial composition can explain 0.90 percentage points of the gap between adjacent and nonadjacent counties in the rate of employment loss during the recession.

These same factors—State location and industrial composition—also apply to the analysis of unemployment rates, which rose more rapidly in adjacent-to-metro counties during the recession. In addition, adjacent counties had a slightly lower college graduation rate, and much higher population growth rates, both of which were associated with slightly higher unemployment rates (by 0.07 and 0.05 percentage points, respectively) in relation to nonadjacent counties.

During the recovery, unemployment rates have fallen more quickly in adjacent counties (table 7, column 4). As with higher-population-density counties, this can be explained in large part by the effect of mean reversion, whereby unemployment rates are now falling fastest in the counties where

---

[16]There is considerable overlap between the group of low-density counties and the nonadjacent counties, but the measures are by no means identical. Seventy-two percent of low-density counties are nonadjacent, but the remaining 28 percent (181 counties) are not. Similarly, 64 percent of medium- and high-density nonmetro counties are adjacent to metro areas, but the remaining 36 percent (470 counties) are not.

Table 7

Factors associated with employment outcomes in nonmetro counties by metro adjacency

	Change in employment (percent)		Change in unemployment rate (percentage points)	
	Recession	Recovery	Recession	Recovery
Not adjacent to metro area	-3.16	1.42	3.77	-2.16
Adjacent to metro area	-5.20	1.71	4.94	-3.19
Difference	2.04 ‡	-0.29	-1.17 ‡	1.03 ‡
Explained by differences in attributes	1.88 ‡	0.50	-1.15 ‡	0.90 ‡
Unexplained	0.16	-0.78	-0.02	0.13
Contributions of attributes				
State effects	1.16 ‡	0.42	-0.57 ‡	0.22 ‡
Industrial composition	0.90 ‡	0.16	-0.32 ‡	0.16 ‡
Educational composition	-0.11	0.22	-0.07 ‡	-0.08
Age distribution	0.01	-0.10	-0.01	-0.01
Population growth in prior period	-0.05	0.05	-0.05 ‡	0.00
Outcome in prior period*	-0.02	-0.26 †	-0.13	0.61 ‡
Sample size	1964	1964	1964	1964
R^2 (pooled model)	0.54	0.23	0.69	0.65

† Statistically significant at $p < 0.10$; ‡ statistically significant at $p < 0.05$.

* In the employment change regressions, this variable is equal to the percent employment change in the prior 2-year period. In the unemployment change regressions, it is equal to the unemployment level at the start of the period.

Notes: Recession period runs from 2007Q4/2008Q1 to 2009Q4/2010Q1. Recovery period runs through 2013Q4/2014Q1. Sample limited to 1,964 nonmetro counties, as designated by the 2013 U.S. Office of Management and Budget (OMB). Seven small nonmetro counties with unrealistically large estimated employment growth rates during the recovery are dropped; these likely reflect imperfections in the LAUS county employment estimation methodology. See Appendix for explanation of regression methods and variable definitions.

Source: USDA, ERS analysis of Local Area Unemployment Statistics data, not seasonally adjusted.

they were highest at the end of the recession. State location and industrial composition also appear to be reducing unemployment rates in adjacent counties.

In summary, nonmetro counties that are adjacent to metro areas had below-average employment outcomes during the recession for much the same reasons as did higher-population-density nonmetro counties: such counties are disproportionately located in States that had high rates of job loss overall, and they also had higher levels of employment in manufacturing, which shed jobs rapidly, and relatively low levels of employment in resource-based industries and the Federal Government. During the recovery period, unemployment rates have fallen faster in adjacent counties as unemployment rates begin to revert to their means, but the net increase in unemployment they have experienced since the end of 2007 is still larger than that experienced by more rural, nonadjacent counties.

Employment Outcomes Vary in Counties With Large Minority Populations

Table 5 also looks at nonmetro counties in which more than one-quarter of the population self-identified in the 2000 Census as either African-American, Hispanic (of any self-ascribed race), or Native American,[17] compared to counties that did not have such large numbers of racial or ethnic minorities. Rural counties with large African-American population shares are located in the South and South Atlantic regions (fig. 11). These counties saw employment fall by 7.9 percent in the recession and have continued to lose jobs during the recovery. By contrast, counties with large Hispanic population shares actually gained 0.2 percent in employment, on average, during the recession and have continued to grow by 4.6 percent since then. These below-average employment outcomes in nonmetro counties with large African-American populations and above-average outcomes in nonmetro counties with large Hispanic populations are striking legacies of the recession.

Table 8 tries to explain these differences in employment growth, with limited success. We compare nonmetro counties with large African-American or Hispanic population shares to all nonmetro

Figure 11

Nonmetro counties with large minority population shares

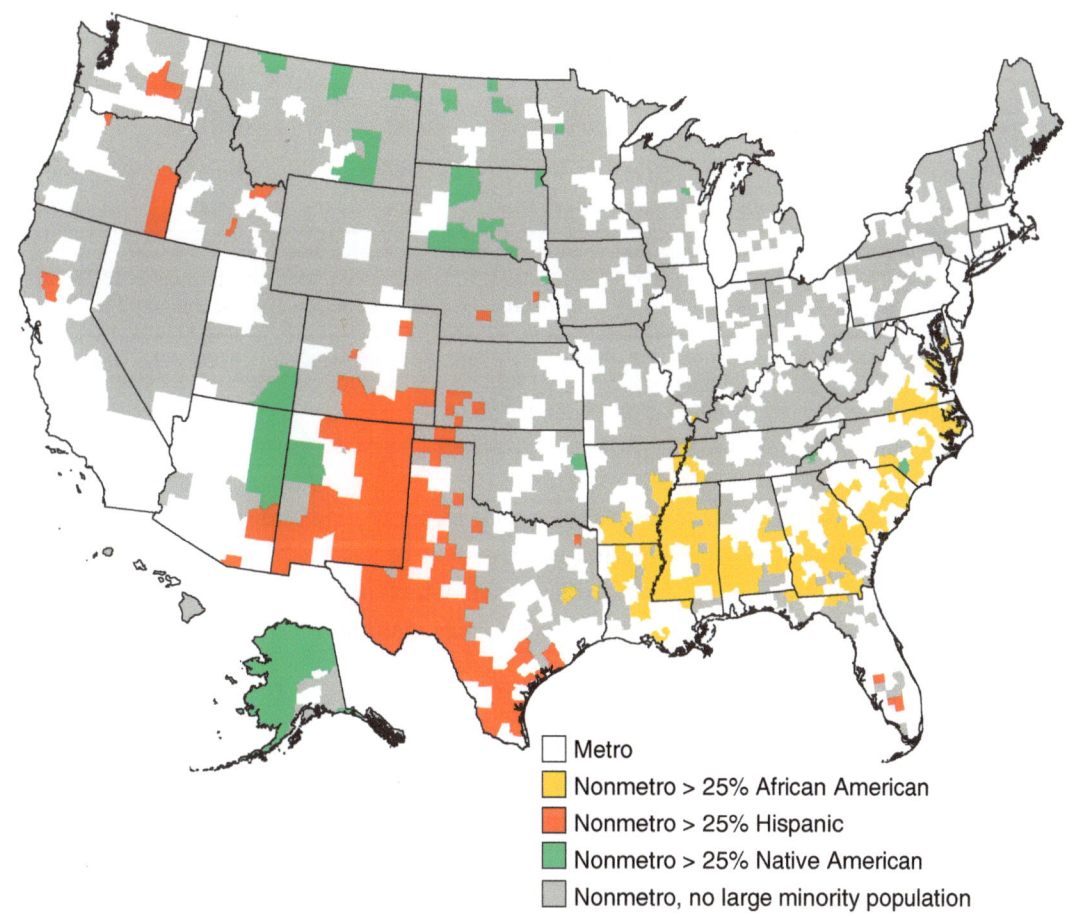

Metro

Nonmetro > 25% African American

Nonmetro > 25% Hispanic

Nonmetro > 25% Native American

Nonmetro, no large minority population

Source: USDA, Economic Research Service analysis of U.S. Census 2000.

---

[17]No further analysis was performed on counties with high Native American population shares due to the limitations associated with small sample size.

Table 8

Analysis of differences in labor market outcomes between counties with large minority populations and rest of nonmetro counties

	>25% African American: Change in employment (percent)		>25% Hispanic Change in unemployment rate (percentage points)	
	Recession	Recovery	Recession	Recovery
>25% African American	-7.91	-1.36	na	na
>25% Hispanic	na	na	0.23	4.64
No large minority population	-4.08	1.80	-4.08	1.80
Difference	-3.82 ‡	-3.16 ‡	4.31 ‡	2.84
Explained by differences in attributes	-3.89 ‡	-2.81 ‡	4.86 ‡	2.41
Unexplained	0.06	-0.35	-0.54	0.43
Contributions of attributes				
State effects	-2.21 ‡	-0.19	1.65	-1.04
Minority population shares	-1.28 ‡	-1.33	1.72 ‡	3.70 †
Industrial composition	-0.17	0.03	1.61 ‡	1.21 †
Educational composition	-0.22	-1.66 ‡	0.06	-1.84 ‡
Age distribution	0.00	0.29	0.03	0.28
Population growth in prior period	-0.01	-0.31	0.00	0.70 ‡
Employment growth in prior period	0.00	0.36	-0.21 ‡	-0.60 †
Sample size	1792	1792	1674	1674
R^2 (pooled model)	0.54	0.26	0.54	0.24

† Statistically significant at $p < 0.10$; ‡ statistically significant at $p < 0.05$.
Notes: Recession period runs from 2007Q4/2008Q1 to 2009Q4/2010Q1. Recovery period runs through 2013Q4/2014Q1. Sample limited to nonmetro counties with large African-American or Hispanic population shares, compared to those with no large minority populations; nonmetro classification as designated by the 2013 U.S. Office of Management and Budget (OMB). Seven small nonmetro counties with unrealistically large estimated employment growth rates during the recovery are dropped; these likely reflect imperfections in the LAUS county employment estimation methodology. See Appendix for explanation of regression methods and variable definitions.

Source: USDA, ERS analysis of Local Area Unemployment Statistics data, not seasonally adjusted.

counties for which no racial or ethnic minority accounted for more than one-quarter of the population. This comparative approach does not permit us to analyze or test for labor market discrimination on the basis of race or ethnicity at the individual level, which is not the goal of this analysis. Instead, we are looking for broad county-level characteristics that might explain the observed differences in employment outcomes.

Interestingly, although there are significant differences in industry mix and in the age and educational structure of counties with large African-American population shares and the comparison group, these factors (which play powerful explanatory roles in some of the other comparisons reported in this analysis) were not associated with the larger job losses in counties with large African-American populations. Instead, we find that the effects of State location explain much of the relative disadvantage of counties with large African-American populations, accounting for 2.21 percentage points of the 3.82-percent gap in employment changes between these counties and the comparison group. In other words, counties with large African-American populations lost more jobs in part because they are located in States that experienced greater job losses during the recession, both in counties with and without large minority population shares. For example, in Georgia the 57 nonmetro counties in which more than one-quarter of the population was African-American experienced an average employment loss of 10.1 percent during the recession; but the 28 nonmetro Georgia counties that did not have large minority populations lost a similar share of employment, at 9.8 percent.

Still, when we include a county-level variable that measures the share of the population that is African-American, this variable is statistically associated with an average 1.3 percentage points of the excess job losses experienced by these counties. The causal mechanism behind this result is not clear. In particular, these results are not direct evidence of racial discrimination in the labor market, which cannot be assessed using county-level analysis such as this. Instead, race may be serving as a proxy for other measures of socioeconomic and labor market disadvantage that led to below-average employment outcomes during the recession. Regardless, these results provide evidence of a disparate impact of the recession on areas with large African-American populations, holding a number of other important factors equal.

For nonmetro counties with large Hispanic populations, State location effects on employment were positive (although statistically insignificant). Three-fifths of these counties were in Texas, which experienced above-average employment changes during the recession. Employment in the average nonmetro Texas county actually grew by 1.4 percent during the recession, and in nonmetro Texas counties with large Hispanic populations, it grew by 2.6 percent. The apparently positive effect of State location was augmented by a positive effect of industrial composition, which added 1.61 percentage points to relative employment growth for counties with large Hispanic populations. In particular, these counties had far less exposure to the collapse of the manufacturing sector, since their initial employment share in manufacturing was just 5 percent, compared to 13 percent for the comparison counties that lacked large minority populations. Another sizable portion of the gap in job losses during the recession (1.72 percentage points) is "explained" by the share of the population that was Hispanic, which was statistically associated with better employment outcomes; again, the reasons for this association are not elucidated by the model.

During the recovery, nonmetro counties with large African-American populations have continued to lag in terms of employment growth (by 3.16 percentage points), and nonmetro counties with large Hispanic populations appear to continue to outperform the comparison group of counties (by 2.84 points, although this difference was not statistically significant). In both types of counties, however, low levels of education have emerged as a critical barrier to job growth. The model suggests that low levels of education have slowed employment growth in counties with large African-American population shares by 1.66 percentage points over the past 4 years, and reduced employment growth in counties with large Hispanic populations by 1.84 percentage points over the same period.

Conclusions

The effects of the economic crisis of 2007-09 are still with us: the share of adults who are employed is at its lowest level since the early 1980s. This represents an ongoing employment and income squeeze for millions of American families, which could have lasting effects on their financial and personal well-being, as well as on their future ability to contribute productively to economic activity. While all areas of the country were affected, regional differences are profound, with a more than 3:1 ratio between the highest State seasonally adjusted unemployment rate (Rhode Island, 8.2 percent in May 2014) and the lowest (North Dakota, 2.6 percent).

Employment losses as a proportion of their peak values were slightly larger in nonmetro than metro areas and began a year earlier. Moreover, since the first quarter of 2011, employment growth in nonmetro counties has lagged growth in urban areas. Our analysis concludes that half of this employment growth deficit can be explained by the near-zero rate of nonmetro population growth, but that lower levels of education and an older population are also acting to slow nonmetro job growth. Together, these effects outweighed the benefits of a more favorable mix of industries, in particular a higher employment share in agricultural and extractive industries.

The most rural counties and those farthest from metro areas lost the fewest jobs during the recession. Our statistical analyses reveal that these differences were again associated with differences in the mix of industries that make up the counties' economic base. In particular, at the start of the recession, the more rural counties had much lower shares of employment in manufacturing, an industry that suffered some of the most rapid job losses during the recession. More remote rural counties also had higher shares of farm employment and Federal employment, both sectors that performed relatively well during the recession. Together, these industrial composition effects reduced employment losses in low-population-density counties by 1.9 percentage points compared to more densely populated nonmetro areas.

Nonmetro counties with large African-American populations saw employment fall by 7.9 percent during the recession, compared to 4.2 percent for counties with no large minority populations. Interestingly, this below-average employment outcome could not be explained by their industrial composition or by the educational status of their workforces. Instead, the fact that these counties were located in Southeastern States that performed poorly overall, in counties with both high and low African-American population shares, explains a significant portion of these large job losses.

By contrast, nonmetro counties with large Hispanic populations actually managed to *add* jobs during the recession and have grown rapidly since. These counties had much lower shares of employment in manufacturing than did counties without large minority populations (5 percent versus 13 percent), which partially insulated them from the steep decline of the manufacturing sector. Their current industrial composition is also conducive to employment growth.

During the recovery, low levels of educational attainment appear to be working against job growth in counties with high minority population shares. Our analysis concludes that low levels of education have slowed employment growth in counties with large African-American population shares by 1.66 percentage points over the past 4 years and reduced employment growth in counties with large Hispanic populations by 1.84 percentage points over the same period.

In interpreting this report's findings, two caveats need to be recognized. First, the report focuses exclusively on employment outcomes (employment and unemployment rates) and ignores many other factors that influence economic well-being, such as wage levels, income, poverty, and other factors affecting living standards. While these other outcomes are certainly influenced by employment conditions, they represent alternative measures of well-being. A second important caveat concerns the multivariate regression analyses used in this study, the findings of which depend on the accuracy and specificity of the underlying data on county characteristics, and on the choice of regression specification, both of which have limitations. In particular, data on industry shares are available for all counties at only a fairly high level of aggregation, limiting their explanatory power. The regression specifications are chosen to work with the available data in order to shed light on some of the broad causal factors that generated geographic variation in employment outcomes. They are not designed to capture all variables that could have an independent influence on employment patterns. As always with regression analysis, their precision should not be overstated, and the possibility of biased estimation results cannot be dismissed.

References

Aaronson, Daniel, Bhashkar Mazumder, and Shani Schechter. 2010. "What is behind the rise in long-term unemployment?" *Economic Perspectives*, 2Q/2010. Federal Reserve Bank of Chicago.

Bivens, Josh, Elise Gould, Lawrence Mishel, and Heidi Shierholz. 2014. "Raising America's Pay: Why It's Our Central Economic Policy Challenge." Economic Policy Institute. June.

Bivens, Josh. 2012. "Public-sector job losses: An unprecedented drag on the recovery." Economic Policy Institute, Economic Snapshot, April 5.

Blinder, Alan S. 1973. "Wage Discrimination: Reduced Form and Structural Estimates." *Journal of Human Resources*, 8(4).

Center for Economic and Policy Research. 2012. CPS ORG Uniform Extracts, Version 1.7. Washington, DC.

Congressional Budget Office. 2012. "Estimated Impact of the American Recovery and Reinvestment Act on Employment and Economic Output from October 2011 Through December 2011." Feb.

Congressional Budget Office. 2014. "The Budget and Economic Outlook: Fiscal Years 2014 to 2024." Jan.

DeLong, J. Bradford, and Lawrence H. Summers. 2012. "Fiscal Policy in a Depressed Economy," *Brookings Papers on Economic Activity*, Spring.

Dynan, Karen. 2012. "Is a Household Debt Overhang Holding Back Consumption?" *Brookings Papers on Economic Activity*, Spring.

Edin, Per-Anders, and Magnus Gustavsson. 2008. "Time Out of Work and Skill Depreciation," *Industrial & Labor Relations Review* 61(2).

Gottlieb, Paul D., and Michael Fogarty. 2003. "Educational Attainment and Metropolitan Growth," *Economic Development Quarterly*, 17(4).

Green, Jeff, and Mark Niquette. 2012. "U.S. Midwest Jobs Return as Applesauce Lifts Obama," *Bloomberg News*, Jan. 31.

Henderson, Jason, and Maria Akers. 2009. "Recession Catches Rural America," *Economic Review*, First Quarter, Federal Reserve Bank of Kansas City.

Hertz, Tom, and Tracey Farrigan. 2014. "Understanding the Evolution of Rural Child Poverty." Working Paper, Economic Research Service, USDA. July.

Housing Assistance Council. 2011. "Foreclosure In Rural America: An Update." Rural Housing Research Note, March.

Holt, Jeff. 2009. "A Summary of the Primary Causes of the Housing Bubble and the Resulting Credit Crisis: A Non-Technical Paper," *The Journal of Business Inquiry 2009*, 8(1).

McGranahan, David A. 1988. "Rural Workers in the National Economy," *Rural Economic Development in the* 1980's. Rural Development Research Report No. 69, Economic Research Service, U.S. Department of Agriculture.

McGranahan, David A., Timothy R. Wojan, and Dayton M. Lambert. 2011. "The rural growth trifecta: outdoor amenities, creative class and entrepreneurial context," *Journal of Economic Geography* 11.

Oaxaca, Ronald L. 1973. "Male-Female Wage Differentials in Urban Labor Markets." *International Economic Review*, 14(3).

Oreopoulos, Philip, Marianne Page, and Ann Huff Stevens. 2008. "The Intergenerational Effects of Worker Displacement," *Journal of Labor Economics* 26(3).

Rampell, Catherine. 2010. "Lax Oversight Caused Crisis, Bernanke Says," *New York Times*, Jan. 4.

Rosnick, David, and Dean Baker. 2010. "The Impact of the Housing Crash on the Wealth of the Baby Boom Cohorts," *Journal of Aging and Social Policy* 22(2).

Sullivan, Daniel, and Till von Wachter. 2009. "Job Displacement and Mortality: An Analysis Using Administrative Data," *The Quarterly Journal of Economics* 123(3).

U.S. Department of Labor. 2012. "The Employment Situation–January 2012." Bureau of Labor Statistics, Washington, DC.

Woodward, Maggie C. 2012. "Jobless rates in different types of labor market areas, 2000-2010," *Monthly Labor Review* 134(8), Aug.

Appendix: Regression Analysis, Methods, and Data

The two outcomes studied in this report are the percentage change in county-level employment during the recession and the recovery, and the percentage-point change in county-level unemployment rates. These outcomes are not simple mirror images of each other, because unemployment rates depend not only on the change in employment but also on changes in population and labor supply decisions of county residents. Together they give a more complete picture of the labor market effects of the recession, and we have chosen to focus our analysis on some of the largest and most striking differences in these effects that were observed between various types of counties.

There are many possible ways to study these county-level differences in outcomes. Standard regression methods can calculate the marginal effect of each explanatory variable and determine its statistical significance, but it is often difficult to get a sense of the practical significance of each factor in relation to the magnitudes of intercounty differences in outcomes typically seen. One convenient way of summarizing regression results and facilitating their interpretation is the Oaxaca-Blinder decomposition model. This approach models the difference in average outcomes between two groups, using group-specific linear regression equations (Oaxaca, 1973; Blinder, 1973), and quantifies the effects of group differences in economically relevant characteristics, as well as the effects of group differences in the economic rate of return to each characteristic. Developed for studying the male-female wage gap, the method is equally applicable to the study of differences between county groups, such as metro versus nonmetro counties. The underlying regressions give estimates of the marginal effect of each of the various determinants of county-level economic outcomes. The decomposition accounting then shows how each county characteristic contributes to the gap in labor market outcomes that is observed between the two groups.

The Oaxaca-Blinder model divides the observed difference in outcomes into explained and unexplained components. The explained portion is the group difference in mean outcomes that can be attributed to group differences in all county characteristics included in the model. For example, on average, low-population-density counties had smaller initial shares of employment in manufacturing, and this explains part of their advantage during the recession, given that manufacturing was among the hardest-hit sectors. Our conclusions are based on the consideration of the explained components. The remainder of the outcome gap is deemed unexplained, because it stems from differences not in county attributes but in the regression coefficients associated with those attributes. In this report, we do not speculate as to the reasons why these regression coefficients differ between groups.

In specifying the decomposition equation, one must choose a reference set of coefficients to use to evaluate the effects of group differences in county characteristics. These may be one group's estimated coefficients (e.g., the metro equation's parameters in the study of metro-nonmetro outcome gaps), or they may be derived from a third regression that pools the two groups. We take this latter approach and include an indicator variable that distinguishes between the groups in the pooled equation. One advantage of this method is that the unexplained component will just equal the coefficient on the group indicator variable in the pooled regression. In other words, the unexplained portion of the group difference in outcomes is identical to the estimated effect of being in that group, holding all other factors fixed. For example, in table 3, the explained component (1.56 percentage points of employment growth) is the portion of the metro-nonmetro growth gap that the model attributes to differences in the listed county characteristics, while the remaining component (0.68 percentage points) is the remaining "nonmetro employment growth penalty" that the model cannot explain.

The decomposition equation is given below; for concreteness, this equation is specified for the change in unemployment rates during the recession, in Plains versus non-Plains State counties. Similar equations may be written for other outcomes and for other pairs of county types.

[1] $\quad \Delta\overline{U}_1 - \Delta\overline{U}_0 \equiv \overline{X}_1\beta_1 - \overline{X}_0\beta_0 \equiv (\overline{X}_1 - \overline{X}_0)\beta^* + \overline{X}_1(\beta_1 - \beta^*) - \overline{X}_0(\beta_0 - \beta^*)$.

Here $\Delta\overline{U}_1$ represents the percentage-point change in the average Plains county's unemployment rate during the recession; $\Delta\overline{U}_0$ is the corresponding change for the average non-Plains county. The difference between the two, $\Delta\overline{U}_1 - \Delta\overline{U}_0$, can be exactly replicated using linear regression equations that model the change in unemployment as a function of a set (X) of county attributes. One regression is run for Plains counties only, yielding predicted outcomes whose average is $\Delta\overline{U}_1 = \overline{X}_1\beta_1$, where $\overline{X}_1$ represents the average Plains county attributes, and β_1 represents the vector of regression coefficients associated with those attributes. The term $\Delta\overline{U}_0 = \overline{X}_0\beta_0$ represents the analogous mean change from a second regression equation, run for non-Plains counties only. The explained component of the Plains/non-Plains outcome difference is the portion that is due to the mean difference in attributes $(\overline{X}_1 - \overline{X}_0)\beta^*$, where β^* is the vector of coefficients from the pooled regression. The unexplained component is the part that is due to differences in coefficients: $\overline{X}_1(\beta_1 - \beta^*) - \overline{X}_0(\beta_0 - \beta^*)$.

All models include the following county-level variables:

- The share of county employment in each of 14 major industry groups for the base period, using county-level data from the Quarterly Census of Employment and Wages (QCEW).[18] At this level of aggregation, agriculture cannot be distinguished from coal, oil, or gas production; unfortunately, more detailed industrial employment data are often missing for smaller rural counties. To address this shortcoming, we also include ERS County Typology indicators, which classify all U.S. counties according to six non-overlapping categories of economic dependence, including farming-dependent and mining-dependent. However, these typologies predate the rapid expansion of natural gas production that has brought significant employment to some rural areas. As a result, our analysis likely underestimates the share of employment growth during the recovery that can be explained by the expansion of the energy resources sector.

- The share of the adult population in each of three age categories (16-54, 55-64, and 65 plus), calculated as an average from 2005-09 using the 5-year American Community Survey summary file. This variable captures the persistent difference between, for example, the metro and nonmetro age distributions. These age categories are widely used in labor market research, since they correspond to prime working age, near-retirement age (a group whose labor supply decisions were greatly affected by the recession) and retirement age (who are over-represented in rural areas.) A more detailed age breakdown was tried, and the results in all decomposition equations were quite similar but more difficult to summarize cogently.

- The share of the adult population in four educational categories: less than a high school degree, high school degree, some college education, and college degree, again using 2005-09 county averages from the ACS. Like the age variables, these measures are exogenous in equations predicting shortrun economic outcomes.

---

[18]Industry codes are not available for roughly 5 percent of total employment, due to the suppression of data in small county-industry cells. These records are retained and assigned to a residual industry category.

- The rate of population growth in the year prior to the period under study. These rates capture prior trends, not current effects on population of the recession or the recovery. In many cases, these prior annual trends are the continuation of trends that have been in evidence for many years.

In addition, the metro/nonmetro analyses and the analyses of differences among nonmetro counties include:

- Indicator variables for each of the 50 States. Their inclusion implies that all of the other factors should be thought of as explaining intercounty differences within each State.

- Employment growth in the prior period (in equations predicting changes in employment) or the initial value of the unemployment rate (in equations predicting changes in unemployment). This simple dynamic specification captures the fact that counties with large increases in unemployment during the recession tended to have the most rapid subsequent reductions in their unemployment rates. This is understood to reflect equilibrating economic and demographic responses to rising unemployment, and that is considered an explanatory factor in its own right, distinct from the influence of other county attributes.

The analyses of differences among nonmetro counties focus on differences by population density, metro-county adjacency status, and racial and ethnic composition. These characteristics were chosen because they were associated with striking differences in outcomes among counties, differences that we then seek to explain. These variables were constructed as follows:

- Population density: Population as measured in the 2000 U.S. Census, divided by county land areas. Low population density is defined as the bottom one-third of counties ranked by density, and high population density by the top one-third. The decision to divide counties in this fashion was made because it effectively isolated some of the least adversely affected counties in America, which we then compare to the remaining more adversely affected counties.

- Adjacency status: County adjacent to a metro area, as defined by the U.S. Office of Management and Budget (2013).

- Racial and ethnic composition: Nonmetro counties with large minority populations had very different economic outcomes than counties with no large minority population groups, as documented in table 5. To study these differences at the county (as opposed to the individual) level we classified counties according to whether more than 25 percent of their population, as counted in the 2000 Census, reported being members of a racial or ethnic minority group. "Black or African American" includes people who indicated their race as "Black, African Am., or Negro." "Native American" refers to people who indicated that their race was "American Indian or Alaskan Native." Finally, "Hispanic" refers to those who answered "Yes" to the Census question, "Is this person Spanish/Hispanic/Latino?" regardless of their chosen race category. Two counties surpassed the 25-percent threshold in two of these categories and were reclassified according to the larger minority group. No county surpassed the 25 percent threshold in terms of its Asian population. The classifications are thus mutually exclusive, and when combined with the "No Large Minority Populations" category, they cover all nonmetro counties. Our statistical analysis was limited to counties with large African-American and Hispanic populations; the model could not be run for counties with large Native-American populations due to sample size limitations. In these analyses, we also control explicitly for the share of the population that was a member of each racial or ethnic minority group; these coefficients prove significant determinants of employment and unemployment dynamics, but the model is silent on the subject of the cause that underlies this correlation.